THE CONSEQUENCE OF STARS

The Consequence Of Stars

A Memoir of Home

by

DAVID W. BERNER

Adelaide Books
New York / Lisbon
2018

THE CONSEQUENCE OF STARS
A Memoir of Home
By David W. Berner

Copyright © by David W. Berner
Cover design © 2018 Adelaide Books

Published by Adelaide Books, New York / Lisbon
adelaidebooks.org

Editor-in-Chief
Stevan V. Nikolic

For any information, please address Adelaide Books
at info@adelaidebooks.org
or write to:
Adelaide Books
244 Fifth Ave. Suite D27
New York, NY, 10001

ISBN-13: 978-1-950437-44-3
ISBN-10: 1-950437-44-2

Printed in the United States of America

This book is a work of memoir. It reflects personal experience over time. Although the book is based on actual events, some scenes have been constructed through the process of memory and through stories told to me over the years by my mother, father, and reliable family members and friends. Some names and characteristics have been altered to respect the privacy of those living and deceased. Some events have been compressed, some chronology shifted, and some dialogue recreated to reflect, as best one possibly can, the true spirit of long-ago experiences. In all, however, I have done my best to offer as true a story as memory will allow.

—David W. Berner

"The Runaway" was first published at the literary website Longshot Island, and an earlier version of "Guitar Heroes" was published in *Under the Gum Tree*.

"I tramp a perpetual journey."
—Walt Whitman

*"One's destination is never a place, but a
new way of seeing things."*
—Henry Miller

*"It is always sad when someone leaves home, unless they are
simply going around the corner and will return in a few minutes
with ice-cream sandwiches."*
—Lemony Snicket, Horseradish:
Bitter Truths You Can't Avoid

Contents

First Thoughts

The sleeping bags were scattered about the concrete floor of our home's big side porch, little bodies inside them all. Matt and his sister, Deb, from next door, Jimmy and his brother Tommy from the home a few doors up the street, and my sister and me, each one of us in our own nest. I awakened just before sunrise when the sky is deep blue, the color it turns before light takes over, and peeked out from the bag's opening.

"You awake?" I whispered.

No answer, only the rustle of polyester fibers as Jimmy flipped around inside his bag, turning his face away from my voice.

"I'm not awake," Jimmy mumbled.

Friday nights in summer, my sister and I, and as many neighbor kids as we could gather, slept on the side porch of our home. The house sat on a hill, a Cape Cod in Western Pennsylvania near a forest of wild cherry and locust trees. Three tall pines stood at the entrance. I spent a great deal of time on that porch, playing Monopoly and Risk with our friends, eating grilled cheese sandwiches our mother made, and slumbering there on summer nights.

I tossed over in my bag and stared into the backyard, scarcely visible in the milky dawn.

"How can you sleep with all those birds?" I asked. Armies of wrens and robins tweeted from the trees. I wanted to be like them, up and around, awake to the world. I wanted everyone on that porch to rise and join me. Get up. Chirp. Greet the morning. Sing in the day.

It wasn't long before the blazing sun rose over the foothills of the Allegheny Mountains, forcing those cocooned bodies out of their bags.

"Who's up for Cap'n Crunch?" I asked, leaping out of the sleeping bag and standing before the screen door to the living room. "Bowls all around. Then, we gotta go to the woods. Cool?"

The wild outside was just beyond the hills even though Pittsburgh's hulking steel mills churned only a few miles away along the Monongahela River. Nearly every summer day we lost ourselves in the thick woods where deer and fox roamed; we played baseball in the empty field on the east side of the old Greek Orthodox cemetery where if the ball went into the rows of headstones it was a homerun. We climbed metal swing sets, rode bikes—English racers and Stingrays with banana seats—scaled trees, shot BB guns at empty RC Cola cans. This was our neighborhood, my neighborhood—my home. And it was from the house's porch that I launched a life, a kind of runway to the world where I dove into the day. I loved that porch, my home, my neighborhood. And it never occurred to me in those boyhood years that I might someday say goodbye to such a wonderful world. It was a good place to be from, a town few of those I grew up with would ever consider leaving, a town of stayers.

I, however, would be a leaver.

I was the first in my family to attend university, choosing a college more than a hundred miles away. Carnegie Mellon, the University of Pittsburgh, and Duquesne University, all great schools, all within the city limits, but I wanted the one nestled in the Pennsylvania mountains. My cousins, uncles, my only living grandmother, even my father, to some extent, wondered why I was bothering with such silliness. *Stay home. Get a job. Start a family.* But my mother had other plans. She insisted I attend college. She wanted more for me. I listened to my mother.

For two years I lived in a cramped dorm room with a stoner roommate, and in my junior year I moved out with two of my buddies. We hauled trash bags stuffed with clothes, plastic milk crates full of record albums, a hand-me-down toaster, and a beat-up TV with a slightly cracked screen to a trailer park about a mile from campus. The trailer's pipes froze regularly. The roof leaked. The water heater broke down twice. The rooms smelled of mold. The entire place leaned so much that if you dropped a ball in the living space it rolled all the way to the rear bedrooms. We were in heaven.

A few months after graduation, I found an apartment in the South Hills of Pittsburgh. It was only minutes from the street where I grew up, but this time it was all mine—a one bedroom in a nondescript red brick building, one of four surrounding a large parking lot. My place was on the first floor. At my first party there, I ordered pizza and made mixed drinks with Jack Daniels and Coke.

After a couple of years, I had just enough saved to put a down payment on my own place, a townhouse tucked in a forested neighborhood some fifteen miles from the city's downtown where I worked as a radio host. I had no idea what I was doing buying a home, and the developer and the real estate agent were a shady team, exploiting my naiveté. But I didn't know that at the time, realizing this only when I sold the house at a loss. Still, it was a happy place to live. I bought my first real Christmas tree there and decorated it with ornaments my mother had given me. I raised a puppy there—the first on my own after a childhood of family pets—and I proposed to a woman in that home, albeit a clumsy suggestion. "Do you think we ought to get married?" I asked while warming up ready-made broccoli cheese soup for two in my new microwave.

This is how one built a life in my hometown. It's what people did. They grew up in unexceptional little neighborhoods, went to the same Sunday church services, attended the same elementary, middle, and high schools, got jobs at the mills or the local banks, bought homes near their parents, drank at the corner bar with their old high school friends on Friday nights, and raised kids who would grow up and do it all over again. For a time, I was moving straight down that path, doing what you're supposed to do.

Being fired from a job forces you to readjust. It wasn't what I planned, but it was what I needed. The radio station I worked for in Pittsburgh was switching formats from music to news and talk. As the news director, I had pledged to stay silent until all was finalized. But the change meant some members of my staff would be released and I thought they needed to know what was coming. My boss fired me over orange juice at a small diner steps from the radio station door. I took a job in Chicago, five hundred miles away. I was one of the first in my family in nearly a hundred years to leave our hometown.

Home was now a studio apartment near Lake Michigan on the far north side of Chicago. My wife came weeks later. We found a townhome in the suburbs and soon built a home nearby. My two boys grew up in that house. In a few years we moved to a larger place just a few blocks away, leaving behind in the first home, a wall inside a bedroom closet marked with pencil notches, chronicling, by the eighth of an inch, the physical growth of my sons. I considered cutting out the drywall and taking the section with me to the new home, but I never did.

In all, I've lived in six different places around Chicago—two houses, a townhome, two apartments, and now a third house. Inside each, I have left something behind and taken much with me, each place following me like a shadow. But in time you learn that home is not something physical. Home is what you carry with you. And in that spirit, I have been transporting my home with me wherever I go. I've been a nomad—not those who roam the land to hunt and gather, who follow the seasons' plants and game, not the drifter who travels with his livestock, raising and living with the herd, avoiding dwindling pastures. Nor have I lived the nomadic life for money, traveling from city to city to take on new, more fruitful work. Out of the strictly defined borders of an insulated hometown, I have emerged a wanderer, a searcher, someone seeking a place in the world to call his own—not a plot of land, not a building with four walls and a roof but something more intangible, spiritual, philosophical. Despite being tethered to the patterns of the past—the highs and lows, blemishes and healed wounds, the unexpected and the ordinary—I have been searching for a place where my heart can find its own rhythms.

Many years ago a friend of mine told me, "David, you're a dreamer." She didn't mean it as a compliment. She saw me as unfocused and unrealistic for the modern world, lost in the pursuit of the unattainable. What she didn't understand (and I hope she may now) is that all of us are dreamers, seekers, searchers in one way or another. Deep down we are looking for grounded space, a purposeful self-awareness. Thoreau understood it when he wrote about human longing in *Walden*: "The mass of men lead lives of quiet desperation." He famously linked where a man lives to *how* he lives and to his authentic self: "Man wanted a home, a place for warmth, or comfort, first of physical warmth, then the warmth of the affections." Not only the affections of others—a spouse, a companion, children—but also a tender attachment to his own consciousness. Home is not what surrounds us but instead what is within us. This is the home this nomad has been looking for, the home we are all trying to find.

A few months before I turned sixty, I lost my sister to her lifelong struggle with alcohol and drugs. She was a seeker in her own way, someone who was forever probing for some kind of peace. Her death propelled me to take a hard look at my own search and to retrace my past, my family's past, the strings that tie me to my hometown, and to understand why I became, in some way, the wandering idealist. There's a well-known French expression, optimistic but not overly grand or pretentious. It frequently arises in the conversations and commencement speeches at graduation time. *Vous allez trouver votre place.* The simple translation is "you will find your place." Like so many, I have been seeking that "place."

This memoir—written in a series of linked essays—was born from that spirit, to examine the broad notion of home, how it morphs and eludes, and the search for it—from family roots to personal discoveries—growing up, moving on, returning to, and embracing a singular sliver of the universe. Like many, I have investigated near and far, from my boyhood home's big side porch to destinations around the world and down the street, stumbling and tripping, hoping to uncover pieces of myself in some way through work, leisure, and love, taking fragments of my experiences with me to build something—a home, a place under the stars. And it is the consequence of all those stars that is the eternal search. There is no straight path. There is no map.

The Street Where You Live

It was not the first time my father's nose had been bloodied.

The punch was a surprise left jab from Frankie, a kid built like a St. Bernard. He lived just around the corner and was a regular on Friday nights when Dad's buddies got together to box in the basement of my father's boyhood home, a red brick house at the bottom of the hill. My father and his friends— just barely teenagers—tied clothesline to the cellar's pillars to form a big square, placed chairs in the corners of the uneven concrete floor, and used a saucepan and wooden spatula to bang out the beginning and end of each round. The boys had two sets of black leather boxing gloves, cracked from age, and they'd tie them up on their fists and beat the crap out of each other. There was nearly always blood from a split lip, frequent scratches, and maybe a drop of plasma from a nostril. But my father had never been hit this squarely in the face, and this time there was a stream of red running from Dad's nose and into his mouth.

Dad often told this story or stories like it—stories about his boxing days—usually a tale about a fight with Frankie and all the wild and violent punches. He would go on about how Frankie wanted to stop the fight but how Dad wanted to keep swinging.

With blood on his face, Dad raised his gloves again and Frankie raised his. Dad threw a right, and Frankie ducked. Frankie tried an uppercut but missed. My father swiveled to his left and, falling away, landed a left to Frankie's ear, momentarily knocking him off balance. Dad threw a quick right and struck Frankie's jaw. The punch threw him to the floor. Standing above him, my father wiped away blood from his nose with one of the gloves and then tapped his gloves together and began to rock back and forth.

Frankie looked up from the floor. "I'm done. No more," he said.

Another boy banged the spatula on the pan. The match was over.

Most of his friends knew my father could throw a good punch, but what they didn't know about was his other, less masculine, talent. Art wasn't something he liked to talk about. Only one of Dad's schoolteachers and his mother were truly aware of his natural ability. He never took a lesson. Dad drew from the heart. He once used a simple No. 2 pencil to sketch pheasants and deer on the walls of his bedroom, and his mother, for years afterward, carefully painted around the drawings whenever she freshened up the room with a new coat. On butcher paper from the meat market, Dad drew charcoal portraits of boxers, some in profile, others in the ring, gloves in the air. His buddies knew about the drawings, but Dad never admitted they were his. "They're my brother's," he'd tell his friends. "He thinks he's going to be a Rembrandt." Dad's friends would pretend to know who Rembrandt was.

After the boys were done boxing in the basement, Dad and his cronies came upstairs to listen to the matches broadcast on the Gillette Cavalcade of Sports. While the city choked on the soot and grime of the steel mills, and men wheezed their way into the taprooms to listen to the same live broadcast, the boys took their seats in front of the big console radio in the living room. My father's favorite, Billy Conn, the Pittsburgh Kid, was not fighting that night, but Dad wished he had been. Conn was his hero, the Irishman with the chiseled Hollywood face, the lightweight champ who took on the great Joe Louis, head strong and battling through to the 13th round, smelling salts propping him up. Conn had the tenacity to believe he could beat anyone, and my father believed Conn was Superman. Conn did not win his match with Louis, but that didn't matter. It was his resolve, his doggedness that attracted my father and so many others in the brawny steel town. Conn had only been knocked down twice in his career. He was a man who even when he wobbled, found a way to square up and return to deliver a hard left hand to his opponent.

"Who's fighting tonight?" asked one of Dad's friends.

"Montgomery," Dad said in his now nasally voice. He had a ball of toilet paper stuck up his nose to ease what was left of the bleeding.

"He up against Beau Jack?" another asked.

Montgomery was a Pennsylvania guy. But Jack was the favorite in this match. Montgomery had beaten Jack once before. However, in a rematch, Jack had knocked him out.

"I'm for Monty," my father said. "He's got more guts."

"Yeah, but Jack is the greatest lightweight ever," one of the friends said.

"Everyone loses sooner or later," Dad said, taking the crimson colored tissue from his nostril, wiping his forearm across his nose, and sniffling back clotted blood.

My father lived in the last house on the street before the woods took over. Sometimes he and his older brother would hunt in those woods, shooting rabbits, birds, and squirrels with a BB gun or .22 rifle. They lived with their mother and aunt, his mother's older sister. Their father had left two years before, not long after Dad started boxing in the basement. His father walked to his car one morning and drove away. There had been arguments with his mother, and there were rumors of an affair with the neighbor lady, the mother of one of my father's one-time boxing buddies. The two boys never talked about it, even though others did. There were times Dad and his friend had found each other in the ring together, but when Dad's father left for good, as the story goes, the friend never returned, never boxed in the basement again.

The radio crackled. The announcers bellowed. The boys fell silent and stared at the speaker, hypnotized. For the next hour, Dad lay on the floor on his belly, his elbows resting his hands to his chin, imagining the punches, the sweat and the blood. He loved the art of the fight, the controlled violence. For him there was glory and beauty in the battle. The combination was comforting. For a fourteen-year-old boy who would soon be asked to become a man, to save his fatherless family, to carry the load, comfort was to be savored, even if it was draped in ferocity and flying fists, even if the fights to come might be bloodier than any of the basement boxing matches.

There was a photo album in the drawer of the dresser next to his mother's bed. In one picture my father is standing with a fishing rod next to his father. Dad is about six years old. He's smiling and squinting into the sun. His father is dressed in a white tee shirt, stand stiff and straight, a cigarette dangling from the corner of his mouth. On the opposite page of the album is another photo. It's around the same time, same age. My father is shirtless, wearing only shorts. He's looking into the camera; his fists are in the defensive pose of a boxer, up around his face. He's scowling.

"Which picture is the real you?" his mother once asked.

"Both," Dad said.

After Dad's father left, his mother didn't look at the album much.

"Don't you wish we could see this fight?" Frankie asked as the voices on the radio proclaimed the winner of the match: Montgomery in the 10th. "Even just some pictures."

"The Millers have a television," Dad said. "But I don't think they show the fights."

"Let's take our own," Frankie said.

My father ran to get the family camera from the cabinet in the hallway. He fiddled with the knobs, uncertain if there was film inside.

"You remember how to work it?" Frankie asked.

Dad was unsure.

"See if you can get it going," Frankie said. "I'll be Jack. You be Montgomery."

After a few minutes, Dad was certain he'd figured out the camera. He showed another one of the friends how to look through the viewfinder, where to push the button.

Frankie ran to the basement to get the gloves. He slipped one pair on as he threw the other pair to my father. The boys stood close and put up their dukes. Frankie sneered, and Dad showed his teeth, snarling like an alley dog.

"Point the camera," Dad said through his teeth. "Take it."

Shhclick.

Dad snatched the camera from his friend and advanced the lever. "One more time," he said.

My father and Frankie returned to their poses

Shhclick. Shhclick.

"When can you get the film developed?" Frankie asked

"I'll have to ask my mom," Dad said.

'You think they really looked like that?" Frankie asked, considering the poses they struck.

"Of course they did," Dad said. "Mean and nasty."

"Like they wanted to beat the shit out of someone," Frankie said.

"Shhh," Dad sighed.

"Your mom can't hear us in here," Frankie said. "She's in the kitchen, smoking." The boys could smell the fresh lighting of a Parliament.

"Just don't say that," my father insisted, revealing the strictness of his Catholic upbringing.

Dad, his mother, and aunt attended mass at St. Sylvester's Catholic Church every Sunday morning. His mother wore a bonnet and white gloves. His aunt carried an old, leather Jerusalem Bible. Dad wore a white shirt and black tie, tight and awkward around his heck. He remembered sitting on rigid wooden pews. No one at the services smiled. Church was not a place for happiness. His family was Irish. The Irish believed church was serious business.

"Shit, shit, shit, shit," Frankie whispered.

The other boys giggled.

"Young men!" Dad's mother hollered from the kitchen. "Getting a little rambunctious in there."

My father glared at his friends.

"I think it's time to head home," his mother said.

"But all the fights aren't over yet," Dad pleaded.

His mother was now standing at the entranceway to the kitchen. "There will be other Friday nights."

Dad turned off the radio and walked his buddies to the front door. It was sad to watch them go.

Three strays in one week.

The first was an old tabby cat with a knick out of its tail. Her father would have none of it, however, and tossed the cat from the second floor back porch over the railing and into the woods. "No damn cats," he snapped. He tolerated my mother's love of wayward animals, but he wasn't about to allow any cats in his home. The second was a scrawny mutt with coarse gray and black hair covering its eyes. Mom's father fed him some chicken parts in a soup dish on the kitchen floor, but the dog didn't stick around and was gone the next morning. The third stray appeared to be a mix between a Boston bull terrier and a beagle, a combination doomed for awkwardness.

"He'll do, if no one claims him," her father said. "And that's the only way it goes."

"What if someone does want him back?" my mother asked.

"Then we give him back. What if it was your dog?"

"But I really like him."

"He probably has a home somewhere," her father said, sipping from a can of Duquesne beer, a hometown pilsner made at a brewery near the Monongahela River. "Still, he has no collar and no tag. We'll see what your mother says."

Mom stroked the dog's back as it gnawed at what her father had offered it—chicken gristle and small pieces of fat.

"Hell, he probably hasn't had anything that good in a long while," her father said, taking another taste of beer.

My mother was unable to leave animals alone. Any dog or cat left alone on the streets was hers. Collars and tags did not matter. Ownership did not matter. She'd spot the animal on her walk from school, find herself petting it, and soon carrying it or calling it to follow her home. She thought of herself as a pied piper, a rescuer. But mostly it was a selfish act. She once had her own dog, a mix of spaniel and Labrador. Tippy was its name. It died of distemper.

"When he's done here, put a leash on him, and walk him around the block," her father insisted. "Let's see if he's lost."

My mother nodded reluctantly. She'd been asked before to do this sort of thing.

Mom put the old leash—one that remained from the Tippy days—around the dog's neck and twisted the long end through the clasp to secure it.

"Come on, Mickey," she said.

"You've named him already?" her father asked.

My mother walked the dog through the small dining room and living area and out the door to the front porch. She stood on the top of the three cement steps heading toward the sidewalk.

"You got another one?" It was the question my mother remembered Jacqueline, her sister, asking. She was in the yard with a friend, making yellow bouquets from the dandelions in the lawn.

"Yep," Gloria said.

Jacqueline had been just as much a dognapper as Gloria. One time she hid a beagle mix in the home's coal cellar. She stuffed food from the dinner table under her shirt and snuck it to the dog until her mother heard its muffled bark. There was an unspoken competition between Gloria and Jacqueline. Which one could rescue the most strays?

"That's not smart," Jacqueline said, scolding her. "It's someone else's dog, you know? You shouldn't have it. It's not yours." She, my mother thought, was repeating a lesson she had learned after her mother found the beagle.

"Maybe it is," Gloria said. "Maybe no one wants him."

My mother recalled Jacqueline giggling at this statement.

Mom guided the dog down the steps to the street. When the road dipped and curved, and she was out Jacqueline's sight, she abandoned the sidewalk and turned to the woods along a dirt path toward a small stream. She sat behind a large wild cherry tree and held the dog close, eventually pulling it to her lap. My mother stayed there until she heard her father's sharp whistle, calling her to come home for dinner.

Mom's mother had made thinly cut pork chops, fried in ketchup and onions in an iron skillet, a frequent dish.

"Can we give him the bones?" Gloria asked.

"I don't see why not," her mother said.

"Dogs shouldn't eat pork bones," her father said. "Too soft. They splinter. They'll choke."

"We'll find him something else," her mother said.

"Did you walk him along Hazelhurst Street? On Willet Road, too?" her father asked.

My mother nodded.

"No takers?" her father asked.

Mom shook her head.

"You sure?"

"Uh huh."

Jacqueline crossed her arms and leaned back in her chair. My mother recalled her sister's accusatory words. "She didn't walk him anywhere," Jacqueline said. "She sat in the woods the whole time."

"Jesus, Mary, and Joseph," her father barked, pounding a fist on the table, his beer can wobbling, nearly tipping over. "What the hell are we going to do with you? Goddamn it!"

Her father stood from the table and pushed back his chair. "Where is the damn dog? I'll do it myself." He marched into the kitchen and found the dog resting on a pile of old towels Gloria had fashioned into a bed. Her father huffed, picked up the dog, and carried it in his arms, glaring at my mother. "You just can't go around stealing dogs." He snatched the keys to his Jeep from the small table in the entranceway and left, the wooden screen door slapping the doorjamb as he exited.

My mother's home sat on the knoll where the street dipped down the hill, about a tenth of a mile from my father's home. It too was brick, but Mom's home was a two-flat, one floor on top of the other with a small basement. Her English grandmother, her father's mother, complete with a heavy accent, lived upstairs. On the first floor, Mom shared a small bedroom with her sister. Her parents' room was next to theirs. Her mother worked part time at the Hilton Hotel in the city, selling cigarettes and cigars. Her father drove a truck for the city's biggest grocer, Kroger. When the government began rationing during the war, Mom's father sometimes slipped a few extra pounds of butter in his Jeep. He knocked on neighbors' doors and left butter boxes on their stoops. He did the same with bags of sugar.

Mom's father returned without the dog. "It belongs to a family on Churchview Avenue," he said, walking past his wife to the kitchen. "They don't deserve him," he added, opening the refrigerator to grab a beer. "I told them the dog needs to see a vet and that I'd be back for it if they didn't do something about it."

"Is it sick?" my mother asked.

"Dog's got fleas, you saw that. And there's a sore on its belly. I'm sure you saw that eye? It's swollen and red," he said, using an opener on the beer can.

Mom's mother nodded toward the girls' bedroom.

When my mother heard the knock on the door, she knew it was her father.

"The dog is back home," he said, standing at the entrance to the bedroom.

"Okay." Mom was on her bed, her head in a book.

"He seemed happy," he said.

"I hope so," Mom said, still not looking up.

Her father paused, placed the open beer can on a tall dresser, and moved closer. He placed a hand under her chin and tilted her head back so her eyes were on his. "You can't save them all."

"Okay," she said.

"No more," he said.

"No more, Daddy."

Dad's mother placed a wooden chair in the middle of the kitchen and told him to sit.

"How long is this gonna take?" he asked. Dad was dressed in dungarees and a white tee shirt, the clothes he always wore to school.

His mother pointed at the chair with a long tapered black comb, keeping her eyes on her son. "Just sit. You are overdue."

Dad dropped in the seat and crossed his arms.

"But don't I get a haircut when school *starts*, not when it ends?" he asked. There was about a week left in the school year.

Dad's mother draped a towel around his neck and dipped the comb into a clear glass of water to dampen it. "It's getting hotter. You're sweating." She stood behind him and moved the comb through his thick auburn hair from the forehead to his crown.

"I'm gonna miss the guys," Dad said.

The sun of the early June morning shone through the window and on to Dad's Jeepers, a hand-me-down pair from his brother, a gift from their uncle who had money. The shoes were scuffed around the toes, the white trim now gray, and the black canvas on the right shoe, torn. Norman wiggled his feet to watch the sun reflect off the metal grommets.

"Can I get new shoes?" my father asked.

Dad could hear the slice of the scissors close to his right ear. A clump of wet hair fell to his shoulders.

"Your shoes are fine," his mother said without looking at them. "Don't move around so much."

She snipped another clump of hair. It landed on the black and white tile floor.

"But they're old," he said.

"Are there holes in them? No."

More hair dropped from Dad's head.

"I walk up and down the hills, Mom. All the time. My feet hurt."

"We'll get you some thick socks," she said. "Hold still." She wet the comb and ran it along the side of my father's head just above the left ear.

Dad delivered *The Pittsburgh Press* every afternoon and again on Sunday mornings. He had had the paper route for several years, over a hundred customers. He knew every house, the names of the people in them, who had dogs and who didn't and which ones were most likely to bite. My father had been nipped a number of times over the years, twice by the same dog. Dad had a way with dogs just not all of them.

He looked at the wall clock above the stove. "I gotta go."

"Hold on," his mother said. She clipped another clump of hair around the back of his neck, stepped away to look at her work, snipped one last unruly strand, and placed the scissors on the kitchen table. "Okay. That'll do."

Dad flipped the towel from his shoulders and quickly stood, brushing away the locks that had landed on his lap. He then tilted forward and shook his head.

"Book bag," his mother reminded him.

Dad snatched the canvas bag from the hook on the basement door and rushed out the back door.

"Bye," she said, standing at the screen door, watching my father run around the two large maples in the yard and hurdle the stone steps to the street.

My mother sat quietly on the front cement porch steps, reading and waiting for her friends. She had borrowed *A Tree Grows in Brooklyn* from the library the week before. There was another book in her school bag, *The Boxcar Children,* which she started a couple of days ago.

"Do you have your lunch?" her father asked, standing on the porch behind her, ready to leave for work. He lit a cigarette.

"I do," my mother said.

"You and the girls need a ride?"

"We're okay."

He stepped to the walkway, toward the gravel driveway and his Jeep.

"Get your head out of the book now and then, will you?"

My mother smiled.

Her father laughed, blowing smoke out the corner of his mouth. He waved from the Jeep as he backed it out to the street, and Mom watched as he drove up the hill, the Jeep lurching as he shifted gears.

Two of Gloria's friends stood on the opposite side of the street near the corner and the sewer drain.

"Come on!" one of them shouted, the other waving her hand.

The two girls wore plaid skirts and white blouses. They weren't identical outfits; the girls were not attending Catholic school but simply dressed in the fashion of the day. My mother wore the same. The girls had their hair pulled back in ponytails, but Mom's dark brown hair hung loose to her shoulders, a blue headband tied in a bow on top of her head and just behind her ears. She was as thin as a novella, like her mother.

My mother finished the last sentence in the paragraph and dog-eared the page. She grabbed her school bag and stood, straightened her skirt, and adjusted her hairband.

"Why do you never see us?" the one girl asked as she crossed the street.

"We always have to call you," the other said.

"Sorry," Mom said.

The girls walked together up the hill, past the other brick houses, past the fire hydrant and the yard with all the tulips and a neighbor's barking terrier. They talked about how last week Sister Mary had rapped a boy's hand with a ruler after he didn't stop talking during reading time.

"It was the boy from down the street who got punished," one of them said.

"The one with the black hair and the broken front teeth?" my mother asked.

She was thinking of the one who was *always* in trouble.

"No," the other girl said, "that red-haired kid."

There were two. One had hair of orange and freckles. The other was my father. Auburn. No freckles.

"I don't know their names," Mom said, "I know them just to see them."

The girls stopped at the intersection at the top of the hill and looked both ways, their heads moving in unison.

"It wasn't the Berner kid. That's Norman," the first girl said. "It was the other one."

Over their shoulders, the girls heard sudden bursts of laughter. Norman and his boxing buddies were hurrying up the street, knocking hard into one another like boys do. Frankie snatched another boy's cap from his head and tossed it to my father.

One of the girls rolled her eyes.

"Not him, right?" the other girl asked, nodding her head toward my father.

"No, no," the first girl whispered, "he gets in trouble for other stuff—drawing in class, making pictures when he's supposed to be listening."

Norman shook the stolen cap just out of the boy's reach.

"Come and get it! Come and get it!" my father barked.

The boy leapt at him, and Dad tossed the cap over his head and back to Frankie.

"What's his name?" my mother asked.

"Like I said, Norman," the first girl said.

"Not Robert?" the other girl wondered.

"No, no," the first girl said. "That's his brother. He's older. He was in the war; flew an airplane or something."

Frankie flung the cap over the boy's outstretched arms and back to my father, but Dad missed it, and it fell to the street. All three boys jumped for it, wrestling for the cap.

The girls were on the far corner now, watching the boys roll around on the bricks.

"What are you looking at?" Frankie snapped.

"Oh, shut up," one girl said.

"Come on," the other girl said and started walking away, her friend following.

But my mother stood at the corner and continued watching the boys tussle. She heard huffing and puffing under the flurry of arms and legs. When they stood and looked at one another, the cap was back in its owner's hands.

"You guys are shits," the boy grumbled, slapping the cap back on his head.

Frankie put his arm around Norman's shoulder. "We're *shits*, did you know that?"

"Shits, we are!" Dad said.

Then came a voice from behind them. "You got a haircut."

All three turned.

"Your hair. It's shorter," my mother said, still standing at the corner.

My father brushed his hair straight back from his forehead. "So what?"

"It looks nice," Mom said. She adjusted her school bag on her shoulder and turned to hurry toward her friends now a half block away.

"You like her?" Frankie asked.

"I don't even know her," my father muttered. "Shut up."

Frankie stood in the street and walked around Dad, studying the top and sides of his head.

"You *did* get a snippin'," Frankie said. "And you still look like a girl."

"Eat dog dirt," Dad muttered.

The boys laughed.

This is how it was when Norman and Gloria were young. They lived among the rust and grit of a city cloaked in the haze of iron ore, where nearly everyone worked for industrialists named Mellon and Carnegie and Phipps and came home at the end of the day to tidy homes and cold beer. Hard work surrounded them. Pride was the city's foundation. It was a tough town. No one backed down from anything. You did what was right. You did your job. You went to church. You helped your neighborhood. You defended principles, your family, and your home. Life was a Norman Rockwell painting in many ways. The narratives of those feel-good 1940s films were built from the realities of neighborhoods like this one. Steel built the city, and it built the people. Norman and Gloria would never work a day in a mill, but they were as strong and sturdy and true as the heavy beams that rolled out from the big plants by the rivers.

But Pittsburgh was not only a mill town, it was a city in the woods, nestled in Pennsylvania's lower left hand corner, wrapped inside leafy hills and muddy rivers, the kind of land

French and British explorers had found promising for trapping and timber, land they had stolen from Native Americans who had lived there as hunters and gatherers for centuries. That history was all around Norman and Gloria, but they were less like the frontiersmen who occupied the land or the laborers who worked for steel barons, and more like the Shawnee, the natives of Southwest Pennsylvania who lived by the rising and setting of the seasonal sun. Norman and Gloria, like those original Americans, lived in the quadrants of the day—morning, noon, afternoon, and night—often outside, often with their tribe of friends. Despite growing up in a neighborhood that sat only seven miles from the nearest steel mill, my parents in their young lives drew in the ancient air of another time. They lived with less steel and more earth and sky. It came naturally, like how they had found each other, without structure or intent. There were consequences to living in a city like Pittsburgh, the hard realities of a mill town. People tended to default to the patterns of fathers and mothers before them—live on the same streets, go to the same bakers, butchers, and churches. But in the sky above them were millions of stars, and one could wish upon them every night, giving Norman and Gloria a license to dream. He wanted to be an artist. She wanted to write books. In a steel town, however, dreaming was an impractical enterprise.

In the days after their first encounter, Norman and Gloria would say hello to one another on the way to school, depending on how self-conscience either might have been at any given time. Norman pretended not to notice Gloria in the busy school hallway, but other times, usually when he was alone and without his friends, he would meet her eyes. Once he asked if she had brought home any dogs lately. The stories of Gloria's dognapping had made the rounds.

Norman and his friends played baseball in the street and the girls would watch, making fun of the boys who couldn't catch or hit, and quietly encouraging those they thought were cute. Gloria was there sometimes, but mostly she sat on her stoop and read, glancing at the game when she'd hear bat meet ball.

In time, Gloria had to have her mother let out the hems on her skirts. A delicate bow would no longer hold in place her thickening hair. Norman's shirt fit tighter across his chest. He made the school football team, and the workout regimen had widened his shoulders; his calves were bigger, his hair wavier. Norman stood erect with a straight back.

"You like ice cream?" Norman asked after a Friday night game.

"Who doesn't?" Gloria said.

They walked to Friend's Dairy. Norman bought two cones. She chose vanilla. His was chocolate. They sat together on the bench outside the dairy store for hours.

Soon, they began taking drives in Norman's car, an old 1934 Buick with holes in the floor and questionable brakes, one he bought with the money from delivering newspapers. Gloria read stories to him from her books and Norman showed her his drawings, one of a hawk in flight she very much liked. And one winter morning, Norman knocked on Gloria's door, wearing a fur-lined cap with flaps that covered the ears. He carried wooden snow skis.

"Would you like to go on cemetery hill?" Norman asked, his cheeks as red as the red checks in his wool coat.

Gloria wrapped her arms across her chest to block the cold. "I've never skied before," she said.

"Come on," Norman encouraged.

Gloria hesitated. "Just stay here. I'll ask." Her eyes had already said yes.

The snow was somewhat icy on the hill above the cemetery, so it was difficult for Norman to keep his normal balance and agility. Still, he did not fall. Gloria, however, fell several times, tumbling into the snow, laughing and giggling to protect herself from the joyous terror of sliding on wooden boards down what might as well have been a mountain. Norman held her hands to guide her; he held her waist to steady her. He told her she could do it. He told her she would be okay.

Over several months, Norman and Gloria would walk again to the dairy for ice cream and share Cokes in bottles from the machine at the gas station; they would flirt at their school lockers and cuddle on the bench outside the football stadium. They would dance to "Peg of My Heart" and laugh, and they would kiss. And soon, they would share secrets. Norman told Gloria how his mother insisted he take tap dancing lessons as a young boy and how he had taught himself the ukulele but was intimidated to play in front of anyone. He told her how his father had always appeared angry and tired and how even when he left his mother and the family, and a heavy veil was lifted from the house, Norman would still hide away in his room, drawing. It was a safe place. Gloria told Norman how sick she was when she was eight-years old—whooping cough—how the coughing spells made her vomit, how her parents were afraid she'd die. She told him how she didn't like it when her father drank too much beer, and how she wished for a house full of dogs, and how she wanted to write but was afraid to put words on paper. When Norman was about to enter his last year of high school, his mother pulled him out. She had tried hard to support the family after Norman's father left, but occasional odd jobs were no longer enough. Norman would have to go to work.

The first time my father stepped across the framed roof of a new house, he moved with calculated caution. He placed his work boots—heel to toe—on the edge of 2x4's and used his arms to balance his strides, the way a high wire artist does but with less confidence. After a few months, his advances became big and bold, and he looked to the ground only to eye a fellow carpenter ready to hand him lumber or toss a hammer. *I could build homes a long time*, he thought. *Maybe I could support a life? Maybe I could ask Gloria to marry me?* My mother had two more years of high school, and she was certain she would graduate. So Norman would keep working, save his money, and wait.

One afternoon, Gloria was released early from school. She was sick. It was not a cold. Not the flu. She had been coughing—a harsh and deep cough. Once she coughed up blood. Over the period of a few weeks, she had lost nearly ten pounds, a lot of weight for her thin frame, a lot for anyone. Her cheeks had become shallow and her arms spindly.

"How do you catch tuberculosis?" Gloria asked the doctor.

"It's in the air," the doctor told her. "People have the bacteria. Microscopic droplets around us."

The doctor asked if her mother, father, or other relatives had similar symptoms.

"It's highly contagious," the doctor said. "And, young lady, it is very dangerous."

Children with TB were not always expected to live.

"There are antibiotics, but they don't always work," the doctor continued. "I suggest long-term care at a hospital."

My mother did not understand.

"It's called a sanatorium. The Pittsburgh Tuberculosis Hospital. It's in the Hill District," he explained. "It's the best for you and those around you." Her sister, father and mother, and Norman would certainly have to be tested.

38

"How long?" Gloria asked.

"Long enough to make you better," he said.

What the doctor didn't tell my mother was that the floors were cold and the windows heavily curtained and the metal beds dressed in stark white linens, lining the sterile and shadowy communal sleeping rooms, were like ghosts standing in a long row. He also didn't tell her that many who are admitted never come out.

Norman's orders came in a simple sealed envelope. He was to report to the Aberdeen Proving Ground in Maryland and join thousands of other young men on the base where soldiers tested ammunition, big and small. On his arrival, he would immediately hear the snap and blast of weapons rattling over 100 square miles of land. But the echoes would eventually become a common element of the auditory landscape. Still, my father would never get used to it.

"I have to go," Norman told Gloria. He wore a white surgical mask over his mouth and nose, a requirement to enter the sanatorium. Gloria sat on the edge of her bed beside him, her pillow on her lap, her arms wrapped tightly around it.

"They are orders. Orders are orders," he said. Norman put his arm around Gloria, lightly touching the small of her back.

"When?" she asked

It would be two months.

"And when can you come home again?"

Norman didn't know.

"Do you have to go overseas?"

"I don't know where I'll end up," he said.

In a few weeks, my father would pack a single duffel bag and board the Greyhound at Penn Station that would take him the six hours to Maryland and the U.S. Army. And my mother would continue to lose weight, swallow antibiotics, and try to build a life behind the sealed walls of the sanatorium.

My mother sat at a console of knobs and switches. Two turntables were set on a wooden base just to her right. The microphone was on a small boom stand and it could be adjusted up and down to satisfy the person who sat before it. The radio station was closed-circuit, its range no more than the hospital building and its grounds. The station was on-the-air a few hours each day, beginning at two in the afternoon with a break at dinner time and then back on the air in the evening for a few hours. The maintenance crew at the hospital kept it running, but patients could have their own shows if they wanted. My mother had hers.

"That's 'Night and Day' from Frank Sinatra," Gloria announced as the turntable's needle played the final notes. "Hi, everyone. This is Gloria and I hope the music is making your day."

There were a few on/off switches and volume controls. It was no more complicated than her parents' console radio. Gloria's show was far from slick, but the tone was sincere, and she was reasonably comfortable talking into the microphone as long as there was music to play. Some of the patients who had radio programs talked a great deal, telling stories, jokes, and reading from the Bible. One who hosted a Sunday show made it a point each week to honor those who had died at the hospital, solemnly announcing their names over the air.

"We had a nice sunny day today, and maybe you were able to go outside for awhile," Gloria said into the microphone. "The weather tomorrow is also supposed to be lovely.

But I know some of you can only watch it from the window." She placed the needle on the record, and it crackled over the airwaves. "I always loved this song, and I hope you do, too."

Harry James was one of her father's favorites, and "I'm Beginning to See the Light" was one he would whistle around the house. When her parents would come to visit, she would ask her father to whistle the song for her. And at the end of every radio show, Gloria played "Peg of My Heart" for "someone special in Maryland."

The music on her show and reading books from the small hospital library helped my mother endure the eighteen months in the sanatorium. She was on bed rest a great deal. But slowly Gloria made progress, building strength, defying the doctors' prognoses, her body disregarding the odds. She was one of the few, one of the lucky ones. In the beginning when all appeared impossible and as she showed improvement, her parents were always there, visiting several times a week. Norman sent long letters from Maryland and traveled while on leave to see her. He'd sit on her bed, she'd read to him, he'd tell stories of his Army duties, and draw her pictures, and they'd talk about what they were going to do when Gloria was well enough to go home.

"Will you marry me?" Norman asked.

My mother and father had their personal dreams, but they never saw them as the reason to forsake the kind of life and home they had always known. On a single block, a few miles over the valley from the steel mills, along the Monongahela River, a young man had used boxing and drew pencil sketches on his bedroom wall to help forget about his absent father. In this same neighborhood, a young woman fell in love with animals and words and fostered the strength to conquer a deadly illness. In the space of less than a half-mile, my father and mother met, courted, and fused their love. And when the

Army sent my father 300 miles away to test ammunition, and my mother's disease forced her into isolation, their ties to home only grew stronger. Dad never honestly believed becoming a famous artist was his destiny, and Mom would eventually realize that writing the great American novel was someone else's fantasy. Instead, my mother and father held to what they most trusted, to what they believed was genuine—family, neighborhood, and each other.

Five months after my mother was released from the hospital and my father was on weekend leave for the Memorial Day holiday, they said their vows in a Catholic ceremony at St. Albert the Great Church. Dad wore a white tuxedo jacket. Mom wore a veil of lace. His father did not attend, but his mother was by his side. Her mother wore a wide-brimmed hat that the breeze kept knocking from her head. Her father cried as he gave her away. Several months later, Dad would be discharged from the Army and return to his job building houses. Mom would be eating better, have much of her youthful energy back, and would be putting on weight. And soon Norman and Gloria would move into a small apartment above her parents' home and consider having a child they could raise on the same street where they grew up.

The Runaway

My mother handed me a long stick that had fallen to the ground from a high branch of one of the two maple trees in our backyard and tied an old sheet to the end of it. Wrapped up inside was a blue t-shirt, a pair of shorts, and white tube socks.

"And you'll need this," she said, tucking my Flintstones toothbrush into the makeshift rucksack. "Put the stick over your shoulder and you can carry everything nice and easy."

Mom led me to the front door and out to the front stoop. She turned my body to face the street, patted me on the head, touched my shoulder, and said, "Good luck out there."

With a tight scowl and teeth clenched, I looked like a miniature hobo with a rotten disposition. I stood defiant on the concrete stairs. *No one's gonna to tell me when to runaway. Not even Mom. I'll decide.* After a few reticent moments, I stepped to the walkway and took the shortcut between the big evergreen trees in the front yard and down the neighbor's driveway. From the sidewalk, I looked back toward the house. Mom was still on the stoop and now she was waving.

I was mad. Mad that I had to practice my simple addition tables, mad that I had to clean my fish tank, mad I that had to go to bed so early to be "ready for school"—mad, mad, mad. It was 1964, I was a 7-year old, and tired of the rules. I'd miss my dog, but I had to go. It was time. It was an intolerable life, and I was ready to break out on my own.

Part of running away is to evoke sadness in those you leave behind. I didn't want my mother giving encouragement about this decision; I wanted her to be devastated. Cry. Plead. Tell me how much she was going to miss me and how unbearable it was going to be without me at home. But that's not what happened. Instead, Mom was all for my adventure into the big world.

I remember it as a rather warm day. I think I was wearing shorts. Probably one of those horizontal striped t-shirts that all the boys wore back then and canvas tennis shoes with the laces most certainly undone. The street was empty of people, a car or two parked at the curb. I remember hearing birds. *This is going to be great*, I thought. *I am off and free.* My stride was confident and rebellious. I walked with a swing in my step. But about three houses up the street, I stopped. *I don't have any money.* My plan was to duck inside Friend's Dairy, a little corner grocery four blocks away, and buy a pop for the road, a quencher for the beginning of my long passage into the big world. I turned and looked to my house. The view was obscured, but I could see that Mom was no longer on the front porch. *Should I go back?*

"You're home already?" Mom asked as I stomped through the front door.

"Can I have a dime?" I scowled.

"Little tough out there in the world, huh?"

Mom reached for her purse. In a small change wallet she found three dimes and handed them to me. I stuffed them in my pocket and turned and walked out the door, saying nothing.

"You're welcome," Mom said.

I was back on the sidewalk and heading up the street. I did not look back this time.

My fascination with oceanography kicked in when I was about eight years old. I liked the idea of having to go hundreds of miles away to get to an ocean. I wanted seahorses but ended up with angelfish in a rectangular fish tank with a pump that hummed and produced bubbles in the water. In second grade I wrote a story about a Cyclops living in the depth of the dark sea. In middle school I was cast in a play. Don't remember which one, but the experience changed my plans. Now I wanted to be an actor and go to New York or Hollywood. I heard Sly and the Family Stone at a school dance, and the beat made the girls twist their bodies. *I could be a musician,* I thought. *Travel the country playing on stage.* I joined the school band. I played the trombone. Not exactly an instrument that attracts the girls, so I switched to the piano and learned guitar. I started listening to Steppenwolf albums. I was certain I was going to be a rock star. Late at night I listened to faraway radio stations on my little black transistor. Big voices from Chicago, Detroit, and New York came out of the tiny speaker—John St. John, Dr. Don Rose, Wolfman Jack—all so daring, interesting, and millions of miles from home.

The soda pop cooler at Friend's was just inside the front door. It was the kind that let you snatch out a glass soda bottle from a metal mechanism after dropping a coin in the slot. There was an opener attached to the side of the cooler where the correct placement of the bottle and a flick of a wrist would rip off the metal cap. I chose a Coke and took a swig. A small glass case near the cash register held penny candy and packets of baseball cards. I counted my money. Not enough left for cards, but I could buy a strip of candy buttons and a small pack of Necco wafers.

"Where you headed today?" Mr. Friend asked from be-hind the counter.

"I'm going on a trip," I said, handing him the dimes I had remaining.

"I see," he said.

"Big trip," I said.

"You wouldn't be running away, would you?" he asked, pointing at the stick of belongings I had leaned against the pop machine. "Kind of looks like you might be."

I reached for the brown bag of candy he had placed on the counter and tucked the pennies of change in the front pocket of my shorts.

"It's a big world out there," he said.

I folded the bag as tightly as I could and stuffed it in the homemade rucksack.

"Hope you have more money than just those pennies. The candy will only last a bit, you know?"

I placed the stick on my shoulder and walked out the door.

"It's a big world," I heard Mr. Friend say behind me.

I was accepted to the University of Pittsburgh, but I wanted to go where my girlfriend was going—Clarion State, a college about a hundred miles from where I grew up. I had no idea what I was doing when it came to choosing a school. My par-ents didn't either. No one else had been to college in my family. No one on the street where I grew up had even thought about it. Some who'd graduated with me or a year or two before had taken jobs at the steel mills. Others became mailmen, cops, and shoe salesmen. After graduation from college I starting applying for jobs far away—Alaska, Michigan, Alabama, California. Nothing stuck. My first radio job was at a small station in McKeesport, a depressed and sad steel town in Western Pennsylvania about twenty miles from home. But after a few years of work there and later in downtown Pittsburgh, I was hired at a radio station in Chicago. I never thought twice about taking that position—big city, big job, new adventure. The night before I moved away, my mother was stoic and proud. My father cried. It was the first time I had seen his tears since his mother's funeral.

I wandered along Churchview Avenue near the volunteer fire hall, the corner pizza place, and along the sidewalk across from the big Victorian house next to St. Albert's Church where the nuns lived. I'd seen these places from the car window when Mom drove to the grocery store or when Dad and I took a drive to get gasoline at the service station. Now I was walking by them, and they were different up close—bigger, more interesting somehow. It was exciting being out there alone, on my own time, trekking my own expedition. I was just a few blocks from my house yet so far away. I might as well have been strolling the streets of Paris, shopping the bazaars of Morocco, climbing the mountains of Tibet, none of which I had learned about yet at my young age. I turned the corner at Melrose Street near the old cemetery and walked along the chain link fence. It was an instinctual move, as if my mind was on automatic pilot set to a predetermined destination. I was now traveling aimlessly, unaware of my direction. I had made a big circle around the neighborhood—walked a total of a quarter of a mile or so at best—and now was no longer traveling farther from my house, no longer walking away from home but instead, walking back.

After marrying, moving to Chicago, and raising two sons in Illinois, there wasn't much else that drew me back to my home-town. There were trips to see the parents at Christmas and visits for a few days in the summers to see an old friend or two, but I had said my goodbyes and was building a life else-where. My sons loved it back there, however. Nanny's house, my old home, was a special place of laughter, baking cookies with grandma, and animals. My mother always had a dog. My sister lived just down the street and she'd take the boys to Kennywood, the big amusement park, the local swimming pool, fishing at the state park, mini golf, and the batting cages. It was a good place for all of us during those years. But in time, things changed.

When my father died from cancer, my sister moved back to the old house to help my mother. A few years later, my mother's health suffered. My sister took a leave from her job to care for her. When Mom died, my sister took possession of the home, but after the grief of losing Mom and Dad and mounting health problems of her own, my sister lost her way. Depression and a lifelong just-below-the-surface addiction to alcohol crept insid-iously into her life. The house fell into disrepair and soon was lost to foreclosure. The home I grew up in was gone.

It was many years before I returned to Pittsburgh. My divorce was finalized, and my sister was now in and out of my life, depending on what stage of rehab she was clinging to. The boys had grown up and the Christmas visits and cookie making were things of the past. I had kept in touch, albeit infrequently, with an old Pittsburgh friend who urged me to come back to town for a few days and see the Pirates play. Both of us were big baseball fans. Plus, I had a new woman in my life, and there was a deep-down part of me that wanted her to see my hometown, something I'm not sure I completely understood. Leslie and I made the trip in the summer. We stayed in a cliff-side rental home on Mt. Washington, overlooking the Monongahela River and the city. Leslie was surprised and impressed with the steep hills, switchback streets, and the views. We attended the game, had dinner with my old friend, and tried and failed to meet up with my sister who never responded to my repeated phone calls. On the day we were to leave, despite some reluctance and melancholy, I asked Leslie if she'd come with me to my old neighborhood, to Vernon Avenue, to the old house, the one I hadn't seen since it had been sold years before in a sheriff's auction.

The street's 1940s era brick and wood-framed homes were built just a few yards from each other; close enough to see the color of the neighbor's couch from the kitchen window. Concrete stoops led to big front doors. Some houses had newer additions—upstairs bedrooms or closed-in porches that had once been open. There were a few houses that had been neglected. Overgrown bushes invaded broken walkways; chipped paint and cracked concrete block foundations were like the age lines of old men.

The home where I grew up is on the right-hand side of Vernon Avenue about a tenth of a mile from where the street begins and at the point where it starts to steepen. Because of the slight curve of the street, you can't see the house until you are directly in front of it. The house would only fully appear before me at the very moment I was on top of it. We moved closer, and my grip tightened around the steering wheel.

How bad could it be? How sad could it look? My last memory of the house was when my sister lived there alone a

few months before the sheriff's office ordered her to leave. At
the time, the white siding was worn and discolored, the front
door's black paint, peeling, the iron railing up the front steps,
rusting, the wooden sash windows no longer closed tightly,
and my mother's favorite lilac bush in the front yard had been
nearly choked dead by weeds.

With the house five hundred feet away, I slowed the car
to a near stop and allowed it to drift forward down the hill on
its own weight and momentum.

"I'm not so sure about this," I said, slumping a little in
the seat.

"It's okay," Leslie said.

The car curved gradually around the turn.

"Oh my," I said.

I parked near the driveway and looked through the car
window.

"My house." I cupped my hand over my mouth. Leslie
touched my arm.

The three overgrown evergreen trees in the front yard
had been removed to allow the front door to accept the
southern sun. The old white siding had been replaced with elegant gray, the color found on the homes of Nantucket. Fresh
white windows gleamed bright. There was a new garage door
and a new railing on the big side porch. The uphill concrete
driveway had been repaved and a geometric stone retaining
wall kept the front yard from tumbling to the walkway. My
mother's lilac was gone but the lawn was green, trimmed, and
free of weeds.

"Someone good lives here," I said and stepped from the
driver's side door.

The old mailbox had been replaced with a shiny new
one. *Are those fresh shingles on the roof? Is that a newly bricked
chimney?* A pair of fancy white lantern lights framed the front

door. The house number—3138—had been expertly carved into a wooden sign attached to the base of the front porch railing.

"It looks well kept," Leslie said.

I wanted to reach out and touch the old home, to wrap my arms around it, to hold on. Instead, I stood by my car in the street at the front of the driveway, careful not to get too near, as if being polite, sensitive to the home's personal space. It had been years since I had been here—this neighborhood, this street where I grew up, where my parents grew up and never left, where my grandmothers lived, where my friends and I sold apples from my home's backyard, door-to-door in a red wagon, where footballs had been tossed and baseballs thrown, where I had flung a hobo rucksack over my shoulder and taken off on my own. I could see my father at the top of the driveway, wiping grease from his hands after changing the spark plugs in his car, my mother on the porch, watering the hanging baskets of red germaniums, my sister sitting on the front stoop, sipping from a can of Iron City beer, listening to the Pirates on a portable radio.

I took two photos with my phone and texted them to my sons. *The old place is looking good*, I wrote. *I am so happy.*

A homecoming is an overused theme, like the plot of a sentimental *Lifetime* movie, but those corny storylines come from truth, something real. There are deep roots in the soil here, generations in the dirt. Still, as I stood at the bottom of the driveway with my eyes on the front door, I was reminded of what it's like when you unexpectedly run into an old friend and find there is little to say, when all you have in common is what came before.

I drove away in silence, Leslie at my side, feeling now as if many others were right there with us, sitting in the back seat with the windows open and the air rushing in.

Apples in the Chimney

Our home sat on the steepest part of the street, so from our side porch the house next door sat below and the neighbor's chimney was directly at eye level, only four arms-lengths away and an inviting target.

Down the three back steps from the porch, in the middle of a brick patio, grew an apple tree. It flowered in the spring and bore fruit in summer. In August the apples fell often, littering the ground and attracting bees. My mother would ask my sister and me to gather up the ones without worms or bruises and place them in brown bags so she could make pies. A bite from these green apples would make your tongue curl, so my mother had to add several cups of sugar to the recipe to produce an eatable dessert. The remaining apples—the odd-shaped ones, the ones plucked by the birds, the bruised and wormy ones—ended up in a plastic bucket my friends and I kept out of sight behind the far wall of the porch. These were the toss-able ones, apple bombs, Mother Nature's baseballs.

"You have to go underhand," my friend, Joey said, "so it falls right in the hole."

My toss was an overhand lob, like the one a pitcher throws to the first baseman after catching a soft grounder. I had started playing Little League and had tossed baseballs in the backyard with Dad, so at 11 years old and with a little experience, I knew the different ways to throw. But this toss, however, was forgettable, hitting the rim of the chimney top and careening into the tall bushes between the homes.

I chose another apple from the bucket. It was smallish but fit nicely in my hand. Leaning over the porch railing, I pitched it with a big arc. It struck the top rim, bouncing to the opposite rim, up into the air and falling to the shingled roof, hanging up for a moment and then slowly beginning to roll, one revolution and the next, picking up speed toward the gutter and the neighbor's metal patio roof.

"Shit," Joey muttered.

The apple hopped once, twice, and on the third, it danced over the gutter and struck the metal roof. *Bang!*

Joey ran. I grabbed the bucket and followed quickly toward the backyard. We ducked behind the big cherry tree and waited.

Mr. McConaughey was likely at work, but Mrs. McConaughey stayed home, and she was most certainly in the house. We listened for the squeak of the rear screen door. Nothing. We waited some more. Nothing.

"Maybe she didn't hear it," I said.

"It was pretty loud," Joey said.

We remained silent for several minutes, occasionally glancing at each other, assessing one another's nerve. After what felt like an hour but was more likely about five minutes, Joey picked up the bucket of apples and both of us walked to the porch.

"Maybe you should go back to the overhand throw?" Joey asked.

Several days a week, our neighbor's chimney was the focus of our attention. It became such a regular pastime, several of my friends and I had begun keeping score. One point was awarded for every apple that made it down the chimney. The errant throws, the ones that crashed on the patio roof, were not that unusual. And although Mrs. McConaughey had not once come outside to investigate, we were taking no chances, knowing that someday she might. She had to.

Mischief wasn't always the norm in my neighborhood. Still, we had our share. It was innocent stuff, really, but important and necessary for a lot of reasons. We stretched, found out how far we could go, how much we could face, how much we could get away with. How bad could we be without being *truly* bad? We threw burning bags of dog shit on porches, bought and lit illegal firecrackers, burned plastic army men, blew up model cars with M-80s, threw eggs at girls' bedroom windows. All of this happened between the ages of nine and fifteen, including those apple-in-the-chimney afternoons.

In my senior year of high school things got a little darker. Two of my friends were in a film class. There was only one camera, so students took turns using it to make short, amateurish little movies. On the weekend that we had the camera, we staged an arrest. My buddies played the cops; I was the perpetrator. We rode in my friend's car to South Park, a big, sprawling, leafy county preserve a few miles from the high school. They dropped me off along one of the park's winding roads, doubled back, and raced toward me, cutting me off with the car, jumping out, and chasing me up a grassy hill. "Stop. It's the cops," they yelled. "Get away from me, pigs!" I yelled back. At the top of the hill, I was wrestled to the ground; they pretended to put handcuffs on me, dragged me to the car, and threw me in the back seat. It was like a scene from *Hawaii Five-O* without the ocean and the palm trees. My buddy, the car's owner, was also a volunteer fireman. You could be one at 18 years old in our town. In the back seat he kept a yellow flashing light with a magnet on the bottom. He tossed it on the car's roof and we sped off with roadside gravel spraying over the grass and the amber light flashing out to the world. The fake arrest was captured on film, and we were quite proud of our performances, boasting how it might be cool if someone saw everything and thought it was real.

Besides that flashing light, a volunteer fireman also keeps a police scanner in his car. On the drive home we heard the police alert for our own arrests. In a matter-of-fact dispatch, the voice over the scanner described the car—"a green late-model sedan"—and "two young males believed to be the abductors and a third male believed to have been taken against his will." In minutes, red lights flashed through the car's rear window. Two police vehicles pulled us over and blocked our vehicle against the curb. Officers stood on either side of the "late-model sedan." One had his hand on his holstered revolver.

"Step out of the car and put your hands on the hood," one cop demanded.

We were frisked and sternly questioned. It took a lot to convince the officers that what we had done was not real. We were charged with disturbing the peace. The film class teacher came to the hearing to explain, and we got off with a warning. Compared to all that was going on in the world in the early 1970s, looking back, this was certainly minor stuff. But at the time it seemed big to me. My childhood mischievousness had shifted a step closer to trouble.

I was not a punk. I got into a fist fight in the boy's locker room once, but no police were involved, just the school principal. I snuck a cigarette or two. Downed a few beers. Hit a little weed. Still, there were worse things going on in our neighborhood in my teenage years—teenage girls getting pregnant, drunk driving accidents, downers and speed, a physical fist fight between a dad and his son in a neighbor's front yard. My town was not immune to the ugly side. No town is. There were families with big problems—alcohol, rumors of husbands hitting wives, parents beating kids, fathers and mothers losing their jobs. There were divorces no one talked about. These chapters of the neighborhood's story remained under the surface, discussed only behind closed doors. Hidden in plain sight.

It was hard to ignore the Vietnam War, women's rights, and all those hippies. Still, little was said. My cousin was in the Air Force and stationed at the Saigon airbase. One Saturday night my mother told her card club she believed America's involvement in the war was wrong and wished her nephew had never gone. She almost wasn't invited back. Not because of what she believed, she later told me, but because she expressed herself at all on something others would not talk about. My father revealed his eventual distain for the war in a quieter moment. One evening at home in front of the TV, he cursed a Walter Cronkite broadcast on the body count. "I'll put you on a goddamn bus to Montreal," Dad grumbled. I never heard him say anything before that night, or after, about the war or draft dodging. Luckily for both of us, the mandatory draft ended before I was 18 years old. But the decade had left its scars—the murders of JFK, RFK, and MLK, the My Lai Massacre, and Kent State in 1970—while my family and my neighbors said their Hail Marys and Our Fathers at Sunday mass, cheered for Roberto Clemente on the diamond at Forbes Field, and cooked burgers on charcoal grills on Saturday afternoons. There has always been a part of me—then and now—that wished everyone had talked more. But that wasn't my hometown's makeup, it seemed. Instead, it was say little, and don't make waves. Push what was unpleasant under the rug, in the closet, off to the clouds. Don't confront. Boys will be boys. Girls will be girls. If you didn't talk about it, you didn't have to deal with it. Maybe it didn't exist. It would be a slow march out of a cultural conflict born from the residue of my parents' reticent generation toward a more open but more uncertain world. And I wonder now about all that was never addressed in those days, never shared, all the things we kept to ourselves, all that was left unsaid, all those apples that clanged on the metal roof that Mrs. McConaughey never questioned.

Joey and I took our places once again against the porch railing, the bucket between us, and stared down our target.

"Let's do it together," I said.

From the bucket I chose an apple with a tiny wormhole on one side and brown bruise on the other. Joey's pick was less damaged.

"Overhand, right?" Joey asked.

I nodded.

"One," I said.

"Two," Joey said.

"Three," we said together.

The apples appeared to hang in the air before quickly descending toward the chimney. Joey's missed the opening entirely, striking the lower bricks, careening toward the roof's edge, rolling, like so many tosses before, toward the gutter and the metal roof of the patio. Mine nicked the concrete edge of the chimney hole and bounded with one hop directly toward the patio roof. It was the first to hit. *Bang!* It took a bounce. *Bang!* Then Joey's caught up. *Bang! Bang! Bang!*

We ran, leaving the bucket of apples on the porch, first to the backyard but quickly changed our minds and darted to the walkway on the other side of the house. It was a good hiding spot; no one could see us in the narrow space between my house and the opposite neighbor. We waited. Listened.

"That was loud," I whispered.

"She's gonna come out now. She's gonna get us," Joey said.

I don't believe Mrs. McConaughey left her house that day. And during the several summers we used her home's chimney as a bullseye, and apple after apple crashed to the metal roof, Mrs. McConaughey never once emerged. She must have heard the loud clangs. She must have known all the apples from those errant throws were accumulating on the patio roof. She must have seen the rotting fruit from her upstairs window. And what about the occasional apple that did find the hole in the chimney? Didn't it show up in her fireplace? If not, where did it go? All those apples, dozens and dozens of them, all that crashing fruit, and Mrs. McConaughey never telephoned my parents, never confronted my friends or me, never said one single word.

Angels

How Bobby managed to lift himself to the second floor window is not certain. But there he was, his fingers draped over the window's sill, a booted foot wiggling through the opening.

"Bobby?" My sister was stunned, standing inside the home where she was raised. "What the hell are you doing?"

Diane had come to the house to visit our mother, but Mom had gone to the grocery, so Diane was alone. As Bobby squeezed his way in, Diane ran to the kitchen, grabbed the phone, and called her apartment where our father had gone for the afternoon to repair a broken toilet.

"What do I do?" she asked anxiously.

Dad knew about Bobby's problems with drinking and the rumors of drugs. There had also been talk that he'd tried to break in to another home on the street.

"Get the gun," Dad barked.

Bobby had now managed to put one of his legs over the inside of the window ledge.

"Top shelf in the closet," Dad directed.

Diane reached above her head, the shelf too high to see what was on it. She brushed her hands across an old ball cap, under a wool sweater, and found the .22 caliber revolver. Diane wasn't sure the gun was loaded. Still, with two hands wrapped around it and a finger on the trigger, she pointed it at Bobby as he lowered his boots to the floor.

"Di?" Bobby had always called her that. He put his hands in front of his body, palms facing her as if surrendering.

By the time Bobby was 13 years old, he was frequently in trouble at school and at home. Not only was he continuing to steal smokes and beer from his father, he was taking money from his mother's purse and out of the change slots inside unlocked cars. He used the money to buy cigarettes when he couldn't steal them and then to buy marijuana from the teenagers. When he didn't have the cash, he'd get his beer and dope by giving the boys blowjobs.

"What do you want, Bobby?" Diane snapped, the revolver now shaking in her hands.

Diane recalled how his face looked that afternoon—veiny, pale skin, sunken, watery eyes, yearning. And when she recounted the entire story of the incident, she would always remind those listening how strange and out of context it all seemed.

"Are you nuts? High?" Diane asked Bobby, looking for an explanation.

"I'm not going to hurt you, Di."

"How do I know that?"

"Come on."

"Bobby, you're breaking into the fucking house."

Diane said she remembered Bobby looking directly at her and then dropping his eyes as if trying to hide.

"Can you give me ten bucks?" he whispered.

"Bobby? Seriously?" The gun was still pointed at him.

"I just need some money."

Diane had done her share of drinking over the years. By the time she and Bobby were 16 years old and in high school they sometimes drank together. When Mom and Dad weren't home, they'd sit together in the basement, smoke Marlboros and finish off six-packs. When Bobby's father died, Diane remembered Bobby coming to the funeral home stoned. Not long after that, there was a rumor he tried to mug an old lady. There was also the one about giving his mother a black eye.

"Okay, okay," said Bobby. "I'm not going to hurt anybody. You know that, come on." He lifted his eyes to Diane again. "I'll leave out the door."

"You bust in here and want me to just let you walk out the front door like you stopped in to say fucking hello?" Diane snapped. She removed one hand from the revolver and gave him the finger. "Fuck you, Bobby! Go out the fucking window!"

Bobby straddled the sill. "Sorry," he said, turning his face to the outside air and lowering his body out the opening.

Diane and Bobby had grown up together. After he attended Catholic grade school, he and my sister attended middle and high school together. He had lived in the neighborhood for 28 years, growing up in a house on the other side of the street with a father who would drive home drunk every night and crookedly park his car against or up over the curb in front of his home. When they were little kids, Diane and Bobby played baseball in the big open field near the cemetery and later stole cigarettes from his dad and smoked in the woods. It wasn't long before they stole beer from the refrigerator. We lived in a decent neighborhood, my sister would recall. Men went to their jobs each day, wives watched soap operas in the afternoon, people ate fish on Fridays from the local veterans halls, girls played with Barbie Dolls, families had dogs. So, she would wonder, how does this neighborhood produce someone like Bobby?

Not long after the break-in, Diane noticed Bobby walking most late afternoons to the tavern at the top of the hill. Bobby would wave from the street. Because Bobby couldn't legally drive, the barkeep allowed him to drink all the cans of cheap beer he wanted as long as he had the cash. Sometimes, many believed, the bartender would give him a ride to his mother's house. One night, Bobby refused the ride. As the story goes, Bobby collapsed on his walk home and someone found him unconscious in the street.

At Bobby's wake, with old friends gathered inside the funeral home, Diane told the story of the window break-in. Most everyone had heard it before, like nearly all the stories people tell at wakes. But this time, someone asked her a question no one had ever asked.

"Think you could have shot him?"

Diane thought for a moment and shook her head. "No. Not Bobby."

Diane was able to see the innocence that had been buried inside Bobby. She saw goodness under the rot. At the time Bobby broke into the house, Diane had her own looming problems with drink. Beer, and later whiskey, would be the only thing she believed could soothe her. She would soak her pain in them. She would hide behind them. Once in a private moment, she told me what she thought would happen someday. "It's going to kill me," she said.

Johnny smoked opium. At least that's what many of us believed. It was the early 1970s and the kids at my high school drank a lot of beer and smoked a lot of weed, but opium was all Johnny's. It was the drug of other countries, other eras. Edgar Allen Poe smoked opium, Keats was said to have used it, a quarter of the men in China in the 1800s inhaled it regularly, but at our high school, smoking opium was as rare as a teenager choosing absinthe over Pabst Blue Ribbon.

Where Johnny got the stuff wasn't clear. No one just buys opium from the stoner in the high school parking lot. How he smoked it was uncertain, although there was a rumor he had a brass opium lamp over which he heated the drug and then used a long-stemmed pipe with a ceramic bowl to inhale the vapors. His personal opium den, everyone said, was the third floor bedroom of his home just up the street from my parents' house. If Johnny's mother had been alive, she would have tossed the opium pipe out to the street, but Johnny had only his three brothers and his father. It wasn't clear what his brothers thought of what so many of us believed was Johnny's habit, but his father didn't seem to care.

Some of us on the block believed Johnny's dad was a cash register repairman, but no one was really sure. It was either that or he fixed typewriters. My father used to marvel at the man's resilience. "He's never missed a day of work," Dad said once when he saw him on a Friday evening, sitting on his porch stoop with a case of beer. In the late afternoon on the last day before the weekend, Johnny's father would return home with two cases of beer and drink until late Sunday night. He was outside in the summer and in the basement in the winter and emptied can after can of Budweiser or Iron City while, as neighbors said, the sweet, incense-like scent of what they believed was opium traveled throughout his house.

Johnny and I grew up together. Our houses were less than a block from each other. Our families attended the same church, the two of us made our First Holy Communion together, we walked side-by-side each morning to the grade school bus stop and were together in the same classroom the day the 2nd grade teacher broke down and cried. Miss Savage was called to the school office. When she returned to the classroom she was wiping away tears, holding a white handkerchief against her cheek. She walked behind her heavy oak desk and placed one hand on her chair as if to steady her body. Two girls in class began to cry along with her, an involuntary response. They had never seen a teacher cry before. Neither had I. Johnny probably hadn't either.

"It's okay, everyone," Miss. Savage said, her voice cracking. She motioned students into the familiar reading circle in the back of the room, touching the top of the head of one crying girl. Miss Savage sat on a stool in the middle of a circle of chairs and read aloud from one of the *Dick and Jane* books she kept on the shelf near the blackboard. "See Dick play. See Jane laugh. See Dick and Jane have fun." When she paused to steady her quivering voice, one of the crying girls stood and rushed toward her, falling into her arms. Miss Savage hugged her and lightly rubbed her back. "It's all right," she said. I remember looking at Johnny, but Johnny didn't look back.

The early dismissal came about an hour before the usual bell, students marching out of the rooms as usual, in single lines to wait for the buses that would pull up along the curb. For safety reasons, teachers would stand nearby, smiling and protecting us from the street traffic. On this day, however, there were no smiles.

I remember Johnny and I sitting together on the ride home, the busload of kids as noisy as ever. Many of us wondered aloud why we had been sent home early. *I heard there's going to be a snowstorm. It's an early Thanksgiving vacation. One of the teachers died.* Then one of the 5th graders said, "Someone got shot. I think it was the president."

I stepped off the school bus into a strange stillness, not knowing what to make of it. I recall how low clouds seemed to mute every singing bird, car engine, and barking dog, as if someone had placed a pillow over the radio broadcast of the neighborhood, suffocating it.

I don't think Johnny's parents were home. His father was still at work, I assumed, and his mother, alive then, was likely volunteering at the church or at the grocery, so Johnny came to my house. My mother and grandmother were in front of the living room's black-and-white television set, Nanny on the edge of a high-back chair, leaning forward with one hand on her chin and the other close to her right ear, a Lucky Strike between her fingers. Mom was on the couch, one leg curled under her, and like Miss Savage, she held a white handkerchief against her cheek.

"You want to ride bikes?" Johnny asked. It was a warm enough November day. I didn't answer. The flickering lights of the television danced off the glass of the living room window and the sounds of TV men talking filled the house. All I recall wanting to do was watch, to see what had made Mom and Nanny so sad.

"I'm going to get my bike," Johnny said. He walked out of the house and down the front porch steps, paying no mind to the sadness in the room.

All the way through 5th grade, Johnny and I played Little League Baseball together, once we played hooky from school and got caught, and there was the time we fought over the pretty brown-haired girl in our class. Somewhere in junior high we began to drift apart. I would see Johnny in the school hallways and say hello, but by our freshman year we were no longer hanging out. I got involved with the school's drama productions and played in a rock band. Johnny drank beer in the woods. I went to school football games on Friday nights. Johnny most likely drank liquor in his car with his girlfriend. I tried weed. Johnny, it was said, was smoking opium.

I lost track of Johnny for more than thirty years, although that's not exactly true. I wasn't looking for Johnny. It is better to say I just forgot about him. I went off to college, away from the neighborhood and away from Johnny. A dozen or so years after graduation, I heard Johnny's dad had died.

Years after that, I traveled back to my hometown from my new home in Chicago to visit my sister. She had been struggling to care for my ailing mother after my father's death. Medical bills were piling up. Mortgage payments were months behind. My mother was not improving.

On the way to my parents' home, I pulled my car into a service station, and there was Johnny, pumping gas into a pick-up truck. His waist-length dishwater blonde hair had been cut long ago. I believe he wore a uniform of some kind. Gone were the jeans and t-shirt. I don't recall everything about the encounter, but I do remember how much had changed.

"Johnny?"

He recognized me immediately.

"Holy shit," he said. "How the hell are you?"

Johnny said he had been working at his job for a long time, delivering packages, I thought he said. He was married. One of his children may have been in college.

"How are your brothers?" I asked.

"All good. Houses. Kids."

Did he ever see anyone from school?

Johnny named a few I didn't remember. Different crowd, I assumed.

"Kind of miss those days," Johnny said.

I wanted to ask him about opium. I wanted to know if all those rumors so long ago had been true.

"How's your sister?" he asked

"She's okay," I said.

"She used to drink beer with us down by the creek all the time when we were kids," Johnny said. "She was so funny. So much life in that girl."

"Lots of life, yes."

It wasn't the first time I'd heard that. Diane had been the spark friends looked for when the party slowed. She could rev-up a dull room with a joke or a big laugh. She was the captain of her softball team, marching up and down the bench, inspiring her teammates to bottom-of-the-ninth comebacks. She smiled all the way down the ski hills at nearby Seven Springs Resort most winter weekends and celebrated Pirate wins in front of the television in summer. She took her only nephews, my young sons, to Kennywood—the big amusement park—every spring, riding the roller coasters with them over and over again until it hurt to laugh.

Johnny and I talked until his gas tank was full. When he drove away from the gas station, I couldn't help think about Johnny's father, my father, the girl Johnny and I fought over in grade school. I thought about Miss Savage, John F. Kennedy, and Edgar Allen Poe. I wondered if all that talk about opium all those years ago was true, and if it was, how much of it was real and how much rumor. And I thought about our neighbor, Bobby, and his disturbing attempt so many years ago to sneak into my parents' house. Was he trying to break in or to break away? And Johnny—clean and responsible—why hadn't he suffered the fate Bobby suffered? If he was truly smoking opium, how was it that solace found its way to Johnny and not Bobby? Why do some of us make it home and some of us forever wander?

I live outside Chicago now in a ranch house built in 1942. The wooden floors creak; the boards of hardwood rub together, whispering to those who walk on them.

"It reminds me of your Mom's house," Casey, my older son, said when he came to visit for the first time. "Kind of comforting."

My parents' home, the home where I grew up, was a modified Cape Cod built just after WWII. We moved there from a house up the street when I was quite young, so nearly all of my childhood was experienced in that house. My sons still think fondly of the old house. And for my sister, six years younger than me, that house was the only home she knew.

"All I want is the house," Diane would say when we'd predict who would get what when our parents died. "You can have everything else."

My mother would smile and joke, "It's about all that'll be left. No big inheritance for the two of you."

All I wanted was my father's drawings and my parents' wedding portraits. Dad drew charcoal art on construction paper as a kid. He was self-taught. There was a drawing of his idol, boxer Billy Cohn, and another of Jackie Gleason, another of ducks and geese on a pond, visions of his life hunting in the Pennsylvania forest, and a beautiful drawing of a dog, the profile of a Great Dane. And the wedding portraits were in brown frames locked together with a hinge, each about 12x8 inches big. My father still had hair then and a toothy smile. My mother looked like Audrey Hepburn.

Inside that childhood home, my sister had cared for my father in his dying days in the bedroom and later tended to my mother's constant needs as her health worsened. Diane quit her job as a produce manager at a grocery store and left the rental house she shared with a friend to return to my parents' place, moving back into her old bedroom so each day she could prepare breakfasts and dinners, administer handfuls of pills, change bed sheets, sponge wash my father's dying body, and later massage my mother's legs to ease the awful pain of neuropathy, wheelchair her several times a day into a modified bathroom, and rest beside Mom in her queen bed to watch old movies, including my mother's favorite, *Breakfast at Tiffany's*.

"You should talk to Mom about selling you the place before the time comes for a nursing home," I suggested.

"I'm *not* putting her in a home," my sister vowed, "*I'm* taking care of her. She's not going anywhere."

Diane's steadfast belief that she could be forever a nurse to my mother was a saintly ambition. But the time would come when it would all be too much and not good for either of them. Dad had passed away peacefully while hospice nurses stood nearby, but in time, Mom would require more care than anyone other than a professional in a professional place could give. I also worried about the medical costs. My mother's home, our childhood house, was her only financial asset.

"They could take it from her," I warned. "If it's in her name and money is owned, it will be theirs, not yours."

Mom sold the house to my sister for a dollar, and not long afterward, my mother was moved to long-term nursing care at a center five miles away. She would never return to the home where she raised her children, baked Tollhouse chocolate chip cookies, nurtured her rhododendrons and the front yard's oversized lilac tree, and decorated the fireplace mantel each Christmas with Dickens-esque carolers she'd made in a neighborhood ceramic class. She would be well cared for, the eyes of nurses and doctors on her twenty-four hours a day, but no longer would her days be accompanied by the intimate care my sister had given so unselfishly.

Diane visited Mom each day, and a few times a week I would telephone from Chicago. Diane would also call me regularly with updates on what she'd noticed about Mom's condition and what the doctors were telling her. And nearly every night after her visits with Mom, Diane would return to our childhood home, the home she now owned, sit in the dark, watch whatever was on television, and drink from a bottle of whiskey.

After a few months at the nursing home, Mom was no longer able to get out of bed without assistance. In about a half-year, she was fully bedridden and losing her mind, insisting my father had come to visit several times and spoke of conversations she was having with her mother. Diane feared it wouldn't be long before Mom would no longer recognize her daughter. Mom began refusing food and wetting the bed, and her lungs and heart were slowing down. Eighteen months after being admitted to the facility, on an unusually warm early December night, Mom died. Diane and I were at the bedside.

During the time at the nursing home until Mom's death, Diane had continued to drink. Her disability coverage ran out. Social Security was slow to pick up the financial responsibilities. More bills piled up on the dining room table. I sent money when I could and pleaded with Diane to try to work with the bank and to consider a counselor and rehab again. She had promised she would do all of it, but when we spoke on the phone and I'd remind her, she would refuse to talk about any of it. And when I visited, she was either drunk or nursing a hangover. I offered to help sell the house and suggested that she might move in with me in Chicago. She considered this for a time but eventually dismissed the idea.

A year after my mother's funeral, the county sheriff's office delivered a letter threatening foreclosure. Diane ignored it. Instead, she opened up the house to roommates. It was an attempt at meeting the mortgage obligations, but she spent the money on drink and then on heroin. It was only a matter of time before deputies evicted her. The house was boarded up. She moved in with friends, friends I suspected struggled with the same demons she did. She no longer had a phone. I tried reaching out to her old high school friends, but they too had lost touch. "I thought I saw Diane walking along Churchview Avenue one day. She looked terrible," one told me. Every few months, Diane would call, using someone else's phone, and insist she was doing okay. But I knew she wasn't. One summer I received a call from a medical facility somewhere in Ohio near Columbus. "I'm in rehab, Dave. I'm really doing well," Diane said. She sounded straight, sober, clear, lucid. Months later she called again. This time her speech was slurred. "I'm okay. Promise. Really." Not long afterward, another call came from Pittsburgh's Mercy Hospital. Diane was brought in, bleeding from the mouth. The doctor said she would go through detox at the hospital and would return to a rehab center for a time. Months passed without hearing from her, and efforts to find her failed. Then one afternoon she telephoned my ex-wife after repeatedly trying to reach me. "I'm going to kill myself," she told Marie. She was somewhere along Brownsville Road at a friend's place in the suburb of Brentwood, not far from our childhood neighborhood. "Don't call the police. You better not call the police!" Marie stayed on the phone, tried to keep her focused through a long, rambling conversation, and contacted the police on another line. Officers spotted her sitting on the front porch of a home. "You motherfucker, you called the cops!" she screamed at Marie. The police chased her down, and Diane was taken to jail for public intoxication and spent time again in detox and rehab. There was counseling. She never spoke to Marie again. Months later, she contacted me by phone and she sounded pretty good. I thought maybe she had found some peace. But the peace did not last. There was an arrest for punching someone at a gas station, several others for drinking, and another stint in rehab. A year or so after she threatened suicide, I planned a trip back to Pittsburgh, and after several days of phone calls on a series of old numbers, I was able to find her. I asked if she might meet me. "I would love to see you, Brother," Diane said. I believed her. We scheduled to get together at a Dunkin' Donuts near where she was living, and she assured me the last phone number I had called would be the way to reach her.

A few days before traveling, I called that number. No answer. I called again. Voicemail full. The morning before leaving, I tried another time. The phone kept ringing. When I arrived in Pittsburgh, I tried three more times. Nothing. I never saw Diane.

A couple of weeks after returning to Chicago, well before dawn and while still in bed, my phoned buzzed. I reached to the nightstand and looked at the caller ID. I didn't recognize the number, and the caller did not leave a voicemail. An hour later, the same number appeared on my screen and again no voicemail. I tried to sleep, but I was restless. Time passed, I stepped out of the sheets, showered, and dressed. The phone rang again, and this time there was a message. *"This is Mercy Hospital in Pittsburgh. I'm calling about your sister, Diane. I assume this is the number of her brother. Please call. We have a message from the doctor."*

The hospital's emergency room physician said when my sister was brought in, her blood pressure was already dangerously low and dropping. He said they had tried everything.

A week later, Diane's remains were cremated. The ashes were sent to me in Chicago. There was no service. No wake. No ceremony. It is how she had wanted it. That autumn, on another visit to Pittsburgh, my sons and I spread a thumbnail full of her ashes on the concrete floor of section 101 at Heinz Field, the home of her beloved Steelers, dusted a teaspoonful behind the photo of Franco Harris in the stadium's team museum, and in a misty rain, scattered the remainder of what we had carried back home onto the earth covering my parents' graves.

★

When Diane and I were kids, my parents would take us to my grandmother's home on Sunday nights for a family dinner. My grandmother lived with her sister in a house on a big knoll a block down the street from our home. It was the house where my father grew up. There were flower gardens around the big oaks in the yard and ivy growing on the home's south wall. It was a good house, and my sister and I loved going there.

One summer Sunday, Mom and Dad drove the family's green Pontiac Fury to my grandmother's, but Diane and I took my bike, a smallish boy's two-wheeler with a center bar between the seat and big handlebars. I was fourteen, and she was eight, tiny enough to balance on that center bar while I took the seat and steered from our house down the steep driveway and up the hill to grandmother's. We had done this before, so the balancing act of two on a bike was no big deal, at least for the short ride.

In the alley near our grandmother's house, we met Mom and Dad near the parked the car.

"Let's go down Hazelhurst," Diane said. Hazelhurst was the next street over, the steepest street in the neighborhood, a straight downhill ride the length of three football fields that dead-ended at the entrance to the woods.

"How long till we eat?" I asked.

"Soon. Don't stay out here too long," Dad said, holding the car door for my mother who was carrying some sort of casserole in a serving dish covered with tin foil.

"You really want to ride down Hazelhurst?" I asked my sister.

"Come on! One time," she said.

We positioned the bike where the alley met the crest of Hazelhurst's sharpest drop. I settled my butt on the seat with one foot on the right pedal and the other on the pavement so as to steady the bike while my sister wiggled into position on the center bar, her feet secured on the crossbar and her hands wrapped around the middle of the handlebar while I grasped the ends.

"You ready for this?" I asked.

"Go!" Diane said.

I glanced behind us and toward the alley to be sure there were no cars, leaned back slightly in the seat, pushed off, and pulled my balancing foot to the pedal.

The ride began with some sense of control, despite the two of us trying to find our stability, but as the bike rolled quicker and quicker down the hill, control rapidly disintegrated. The handlebars began to shimmy and shake. Diane, seated on the bike's center bar was now shifting her weight back and forth trying to regain some level of equilibrium. The front tire began to wobble. The rear one began to shudder.

"Woooo!" my sister yelled, as if she were riding the biggest dip on a roller coaster.

Her exhilaration met my panic. I put a death grip on the handlebars. Why I didn't try the bike's brakes, I don't remember. Instead, I dropped my feet to the ground to drag the toes of my tennis shoes along the concrete, hoping friction would slow us down. The move only created more trembling. The speed was too much and the bike was no longer in my power. It zigzagged from one side of the street to the other, the handlebars now violently shaking, throwing my hands from their grips.

"Yes!" Diane roared, reaching her arms in the air high above her head.

The bike's front tire swerved into loose roadside gravel, the momentum taking us toward a standalone mailbox next to a driveway. I reached out and pushed off the wooden post to keep us from crashing into it. It worked, but the speed and our weight jerked the bike again toward the street so hard that the rear tire lifted off the ground and tossed us sideways. The bike hit the pavement and flipped. Our bodies slammed to the street, skin on elbows and knees scraping across the immoveable asphalt. One of my shoes flew off. The bike was now in the middle of the street, halfway down the hill.

After a second of uncertainty, I pulled my body to a sitting position, caught my breath, and reached for the raw, red skin just below my right knee. Diane jumped to her feet.

"That was nuts! Oh my God!"

"You okay?" I asked.

"That was so cool! So cool!"

"Your arm. It's bleeding," I said, pointing to Diane's left elbow.

"Did you feel it in your stomach? Did you?" she asked, ignoring my observation. "That was like riding the rides at the carnival!"

"There's blood dripping," I said.

Diane lifted her elbow to take a look. She licked her fingers, wiped at the wound, and turned to me. "Let's do it again," she said.

I lifted myself off the pavement and inspected my raspberry scrapes. "You're crazy," I mumbled. I brushed pieces of gravel and dirt off my shins and from under my forearms. "Get the bike."

"Come on. One more time," Diane pleaded, raising the bike to its tires and pushing it toward me.

I started to giggle.

"We have time," she said. "Come on."

The bike's handlebars were slightly bent, but it still seemed to work. I began walking it up the hill, my back to Diane. "No," I said, half smiling.

"You're a baby," Diane said, following behind me. "Come onnnn!" Both of us were now sharing the kind of nervous, adrenaline-fueled laughter that comes after an unexpected moment of stress or trauma, when you know it's all okay, you made it through, you squeezed out something good from something bad. "After dinner? After we eat?" Diane begged. "Please."

I heard my father's piercing whistle.

"Mom's gonna kill us," I muttered.

Many years later, when we were adults, my sister and I would recall that perilous bike ride many times over. "It was all your idea, you know?" She'd recount the treacherous hill, the wobbling handlebars, and the out-of-control speed. And she'd describe her fear—how her "heart was in her throat"—and how she "couldn't breathe." In the bloodiest of detail, she'd count off her bruises. "All over my body," she'd insist. She'd maintain I was behind the entire thing. "*You* were a daredevil!" she'd say. She'd claim the bike was in pieces, that the tires flew off, that a car nearly hit us. "You were crazy, Brother. Nuts!" she'd say, praising my risk-taking "But, as wild as that was, Brother, I guess I do have to thank you. You did somehow keep me from getting killed. I was hurt. But I didn't die." She'd laugh and I'd laugh back.

I never tried to straighten out my sister's story or remind her that it didn't happen quite that way, or that her recollections were not entirely accurate, and her embellishments had been whisked together with half-remembered details. It didn't matter because what Diane wanted to believe had happened that Sunday afternoon, despite her certainty that I had coaxed her to join me in that crazy ride, was that her brother, in the end, was there that day to save her.

Ghosts

My grandmother died on a Sunday morning. But in the earlier hours of that day, she had been seen walking away from my parent's home where she had been living for almost a year. It was a slow stride through the backyards, just after sunrise, across the next door neighbor's lot and down over the hill, and out of sight. At least this is what my family had been told.

Nanny, as we called her, moved in with my parents, my sister, and me after a series of health issues—hardening of the arteries and nagging heart problems—all related to her love of Lucky Strikes. A cup of black coffee and a cigarette was breakfast. Her cigarette case was never far out of reach. Not until the end did her smoking appear to slow her down. She had a great deal of spunk for many years, chasing my sister and me around the kitchen table, pretending to have a booger on the end of her finger and threatening to wipe it on us. She offered me my first hot tea when I was about five years old. Defying my mother's rules, Nanny snuck four scoops of sugar and a load of milk into the black tea. How could a kid not love it? Then there was the time she stood up to the bullies in the neighborhood. The "big kids," as we called them, were teasing my friends and me while we played on our home's front porch. They called us names and threw sticks and rocks. Nanny saw them from the picture window and marched outside to the porch, rolled up the sleeve of her blouse, and made a muscle. She had a pretty good one, bulging from her sinewy arms. Nanny never said a word to those bullies, just flexed her bicep. The bullies ran and never came back.

Nanny had been feeling particularly ill in the days before that Sunday. Doctors had continually warned her about the cigarettes, but, honestly, by then, there probably wasn't much point. The damage had been done. Saturday night, as my mother later told me, Nanny went to bed early, complaining of fatigue. The next morning, my mother found her dead in her bed. Doctors say she probably died quietly in her sleep.

Walking home from Catholic Sunday school, I found my father waiting for me at the bottom of our long, steep driveway.

"Go," he said, pointing down the street toward where my other grandmother, his mother, and great aunt lived. I asked why. "Please go to Granny's," he said. Dad's eyes were red. His shoulders slumped. I did what he insisted but walked slowly to Granny's house, uncertain of what I might find there. I picked up a stick from one of the yards and dragged it on the concrete street. I threw a pebble at a squirrel. I watched a crow on the high branch of a tree, standing proudly and cawing at the sky.

My granny and Aunt Maggie gave me sugared peaches in a bowl and sat me down in front of the television in the living room. I could hear them whispering in the kitchen, one of them sniffling every few seconds. An old black-and-white John Wayne movie was being broadcast, but I wasn't paying much attention.

Eventually, my father came through the rear door that led to the kitchen. There were more whispers, and someone said, "Oh my." Then silence. My eyes were still on John Wayne when my father called my name.

I don't remember who told me Nanny was dead. It might have been my grandmother, possibly Aunt Maggie. I am nearly certain, however, it wasn't my father. Later in my twenties I learned how sensitive my father was, how emotional he could get, although he hid much of it. So when I remember this, I cannot imagine my father telling me Nanny was gone.

Days later, after the wake and the funeral, my mother was gardening in the front yard when the lady who lived next door called to her from her front stoop. The woman had been to Nanny's wake. "How are you doing, Gloria?" she asked my mother. My mother responded like most do. "I'm all right," she said, although not really meaning it. The neighbor then asked if it would be okay to share a story about Nanny, one she said she didn't feel comfortable revealing at the funeral.

The morning of my grandmother's death, the neighbor had been washing dishes at her kitchen sink. Above her was a window that looked out to the backyards of the homes on the street. It was quiet and she was alone. She scrubbed a few dishes and occasionally looked out to her patio to watch the wrens eat from a feeder. In one of those glances, she spotted someone, a figure, walking across the backyards. At first, she told my mother, she wasn't able to determine who it was, so she continued to watch. *This is curious*, she thought. *It's so early in the day.* The figure moved with deliberate steps through one yard and past a fence and a row of pines to another yard. The figure then slowed and turned to look over her shoulder for a moment. That's when the neighbor says she saw who it was. My Nanny. Virginia Warren was out at the first light of day, walking through the back lawns and away from our home. *Why would she be out there*, the neighbor wondered. *She's been ill. Is she going to the store for cigarettes? She's not well enough to be doing this.* She was right; Nanny was not well enough. She never would have attempted such a walk. The neighbor said she kept her eyes on the figure as the woman, my Nanny, walked out of sight.

"I didn't want to tell you right away," the neighbor told my mother. "I thought maybe I was seeing things."

The neighbor said she finished her dishes, made some coffee, and settled in to read the Sunday newspaper, still contemplating what she had seen. In less than an hour, she saw flashing red lights in the driveway of my parent's home. Nanny's body was in her bed, no sign of having gone out, no sign of having left.

I'm not sure what I think of ghosts, but whenever the conversation turns to apparitions and the afterlife, I tell the story of my Nanny.

In the summer of 2011, I lived in Jack Kerouac's home in Orlando, an old tin-roof cottage in the College Park neighborhood of the city. He lived there with his mother just after *On the Road* was published. In a tiny back room with one window that looked out to the yard to a fruitful orange tree in the rear of the house, Kerouac wrote *The Dharma Bums*. *The New York Times* interviewed him in that room. There are photos from the newspaper framed and hung on the walls. On a small wooden desk near the window, I set up my space for a three-month stay, one I had been awarded as a writer-in-residence. I worked every early morning at that desk on a manuscript, and after a couple of hours, I would make coffee and wheat pancakes, nourish myself, then return to writing for another hour or so. In midmorning, I would break before the Florida sun began to burn and walk through the neighborhood, stop for coffee at Downtown Credo, a non-profit coffee shop, and read the local papers. Sometimes I rode my bike around Lake Silver.

After a few days staying in the house and reading about the frenetic nights Kerouac spent in that back room writing, madly typing his words in the same space I had claimed for the summer, I wondered if his spirit might be hovering in the corners. At the time he'd lived there, he had taken to Zen Buddhism, mixing the teachings with his Catholicism, and had begun to mediate, although he had written that he wasn't so good at it. His friend, the poet, Gary Snyder, had helped him understand the contemplative, inner process, but Kerouac apparently could never reach the depth of the discipline that Snyder had prescribed. Still, he tried. Did the best he could. And I too had tried. I had experimented in silent moments, trying to quiet my mind. Like Kerouac, I was merely a struggling student, a freshman with a lot to learn. But I wondered if meditation might be the way to connect with whatever ghost might be lingering in that house.

One early morning, before beginning to write, I sat on the twin bed in the room and crossed my legs. I rested my hands, palms up, on my knees, and closed my eyes. I took breath after unhurried, deliberate breath, my muscles slowly melting, tightness and stiffness gently lifting away. My difficulty with the discipline was the hard work of forgetting time, dismissing the rush of my thoughts. But for whatever reason, that morning was different. It came easier.

"Jack," I whispered, "if you are in the room, let me know."

I took in air, let it out gradually, and did it again.

"I thank you, Jack, for this time here, this little room, and if your creative energy remains, I wonder if you might offer it to me."

If I had been executing the process well, I would not have heard the chirp of birds outside the window or the muffled engine of a garbage truck traveling past.

"Any sign, Jack. Anything."

I took in one deep breath, filled my lungs, and slowly puffed out the air, counting silently down from ten. I sank my body further into the mattress, attempting to make myself heavy and at the same time feather light. I felt my heart pump in my chest. It was not the thump of anxious beating but, instead, a tender rhythm.

"Jack?"

Silence took over. I remained cross-legged on the bed for another ten, maybe fifteen minutes, I suspected. For three days in a row, I added this ritual to my morning. I stopped for a few days and tried again a month later, a few more times after that, and then one last time on my final morning at the house in mid-August. Still, there was nothing, no sign, not the faintest indication that Jack was anywhere near.

A few years after my time in Orlando, I was offered office space in Ernest Hemingway's birthplace home in Oak Park, Illinois outside Chicago. I was asked to help develop a literary journal for the Hemingway Foundation. Questions are frequently asked about my time at the old Victorian home. Was he really born there? Didn't he famously hate Oak Park? What book did he write there? (None of them.) But one inquiry tops all others: Have you seen his ghost?

My workspace was in a freshly constructed writer's room in the house's attic, on the same floor where it's believed Ernest played as a child. You can't help consider him there. The photographs of Ernest as a very young boy are scattered throughout the home, and one can easily imagine his presence. But a ghost? My office door was closed when I worked there, so if a ghost were to show himself, he'd have to slip through the wall, something ghosts are said to do quite well. It would be such a good story to tell, a spirit sighting in the old house. *Ernie showed up to say hello, offered some writing tips, invited me deep sea fishing, brought me a drink.* But it never happened. Ernie never revealed himself in any sensory way.

Sometime in the early 1980s, I discovered an old typewriter in an antique shop in Zelienople, a small town in Western Pennsylvania, not far from where I grew up. I snatched it up because it was, I believed, the same make and model of a typewriter Hemingway used at his homes in Key West and Cuba. He was known for writing standing up and frequently, if not always, in longhand. But he did type, mainly when drafting his stories, and in Key West the word is, he used a Corona portable. There's some debate about the exact model and whether the typewriter on display in his museum-home in Key West was truly his or a copy.

In my home on a small side table in the basement office sits the portable Corona I found years ago. One night, some months after beginning work at the Hemingway house, I had a dream. I have many dreams, or I should say I remember many of my dreams. Some are more than odd. I call them my "Lucy in the Sky with Diamonds" dreams, including the Plastacine porters. I've dreamed of pigs dressed as Nazis, a knife fight with a fish, and my most euphoric, the ability to wave my hands and create magnificent gardens. This dream, however, was about my typewriter. Someone was snapping at the keys. *Tap, tick, whack.* The writer was manic, attacking the letters. I could hear the *clack, clack, clack* in my dream or the semi-sleep I may have been in. It was a fleeting dream, the kind you experience in the misty space between REM and awakening, but still, I was certain the sounds were real.

Mr. Hemingway?

There was no other context to the dream. No narrative that made sense. No second act, just the typing.

Ernie?

No ghost at the Hemingway birthplace home, but maybe there was one at mine. But why? If one believes in such things, why would the spirit of Hemingway show up at my home and not his?

Hemingway's ghost has been seen in Key West, coming out of Sloppy Joe's bar, and more legendary sightings have been documented at his house there. He walks outside on the balcony, and neighbors say they sometimes see the figure of Papa looking out a second floor window. And they've heard the typewriter. *Tap, click, whack. Clack, clack, clack.*

Maybe this is simply silly talk meant for tourists. Or maybe it isn't. Hemingway owned the Key West house from 1931 to 1961, although he didn't live there for all thirty years. In 1939, he divorced his wife, Pauline, and went to live in Cuba. Still, Key West was a good place for him. His children were raised in the home and many of his novels were written there. Maybe that's why apparitions appear in Key West and not at the birthplace house. It's a simple thing, really. Ghosts hang out where they feel most at home. For Hemingway it was the house on Whitehead Street. For Kerouac it wasn't the home in Orlando. For Jack, home was on the road.

Why, then, was there night typing at my home? *It's just a dream, David. Only a dream.* But after reading about so many stories of those who have experienced unexplained sounds in their homes, noises that appear in dreams, I began to turn my thinking upside down. Why *couldn't* it be real?

There have been hundreds of stories of spirit visitors seen at the bedsides of dying persons. Deathbed visits were rarely mentioned in scientific literature until the late 1920s. Sir William Barrett, a professor of physics at the Royal College of Science in Dublin, became interested when his wife, a doctor, came home one evening and told him about a woman patient who died the day after giving birth. Just before she died, the woman sat up in bed and insisted her father had come to visit and to take her away. This sparked Barrett's research, and in 1926 he published *Deathbed Visions*, documenting dozens of cases, and in each one, the person dying saw someone who had died before them. The visit was usually short, five minutes at best, and it didn't matter if the dying person was religious or believed at all in the afterlife. Many might explain this away. The patients were delirious in their illnesses, they were using strong medications, they might be old and suffering delusions, or they wished for the visit so strongly that they simply believed their wish.

In the days before my mother passed away in a nursing home, dementia tearing at her brain, she insisted my father, who had died some six years before, had come to visit her in her room. I never disputed the visits. It was her reality, and she deserved that. But still, there was the dementia, so some could easily point to her deteriorating condition to explain the visions.

Those who study paranormal activity believe there are at least two types of ghosts, the intelligent and the residual. The intelligent spirit is the one who will interact with you, call your name, move an object, throw something. *Might they also type?* The residuals are those whose energy remains in the place most familiar to them—a home, a favorite bar, an artist's studio. *Hemingway in Key West?* Paranormal scientists say these ghosts are usually confused or cannot acknowledge, for whatever reason, that they have passed on.

There is no hard evidence that totally refutes these stories, just as there is nothing that completely proves them, either.

But does it matter? Proof is overrated. Faith and spirit have their place, don't they, the place of ghosts? What is certain is that if one believes spirits are real, in whatever way that manifests, or that energy is forever, in whatever form it sparks, then it would make sense to believe in the Hemingway sightings in Key West, typewriters clacking in the dark, or a grandmother taking one last walk from her home to a new home with the angels.

My Nanny was buried with a carton of Lucky Strikes. I hope she's smoking slowly. Eternity is a long time.

Gone

I waved goodbye, turned, and never looked back. My mother said she and my father drove home in silence that night, not saying a word to each other for two hours.

We do what we are supposed to do when we leave home for the first time. We stand tall, we rejoice in the independence, the freedom, and we move on. This is not to say it isn't hard, or doesn't deserve or warrant a cry, a dose of separation sadness. But when we walk over that bridge toward our own life from the lives of those who raised us, it is most of the time, remarkable and good. We may not realize the power of that moment until a long time has gone.

I was the first in my family to attend college. I came from men of the working class. My grandfather was a truck driver, my father wielded a hammer and saw in a crew that built homes, my cousins worked construction, sold machinery; my uncle sold steel. When construction jobs slowed in the early 1960s, my father took a position in an insurance agency, but he hated it. Years later, Dad returned to remodeling and working with his hands. I was the oddball in the family. I was the "thinker," as my mother used to say. I read books and played music and didn't much want to learn the skills my father wanted to teach—how to change a car's oil filter, how to repair a lawnmower, how to put in a new vanity sink in a bathroom. My mother knew this about me early on, and she was certain I was a college man. "You're going," she said. "There will be no questioning this." I never considered another path.

It was mid-morning in late August of 1974 when my mother, father, and I left for the two-hour drive from Pittsburgh's South Hills to Clarion State College, my father's Pontiac Fury packed with a suitcase of blue jeans, flannel shirts, Led Zeppelin and Beatles t-shirts, a hot plate, a copy of Kerouac's *On the Road*, *Watership Down*, and *The Hobbit*. I had a milk crate of albums—CSNY's *Déjà vu*, *Led Zeppelin II*, and the *America* album with the photo of the band members sitting in front of the likenesses of Native Americans. My Yamaha acoustic guitar was inside a hard, black case, and a new set of Ernie Ball steel strings was tucked behind the neck.

My parents helped me move into the first floor dorm room at Wilkinson Hall. It was a plain, stark place—concrete block walls, hard plastic doors covered small closets, two metal twin beds pushed against opposite ends of the room, and two desks made of particle board in the corners near the narrow crank windows that looked out toward the dorm's entrance. My new roommate, one I had not yet met, was pulling on a bong at his desk behind the small bookshelf.

"Hello," my mother said, slowly opening the door with the key we were given at the dormitory's front desk. The door stuck for a moment, catching on a wet towel that had been placed across the crack at the bottom.

"Oh, hey," the roommate coughed. "Hi. Yeah. Okay. You're here." He frantically waved away smoke, stood, and walked in front of the desk. "I'm, ah, John." He held out his hand.

"Your roommate is here," Mom said. "Are you allowed to smoke in here?" My mother could not have recognized the skunk-like smell of marijuana, but the smoke was not to be missed.

"Well, I guess not," the roommate said. "I probably shouldn't, you know?"

I put my guitar case against the wall and placed the box I'd stuffed with books, a clock radio, a coffee mug, and the hot plate on one of the beds.

"I hope you don't mind," the roommate said, pointing to the blankets strewn across the other bed. "I just picked one."

"I'm Dave," I said, shaking his hand. "It doesn't matter to me, man."

Dad trailed behind us and walked in the room a couple minutes later, carrying a duffel bag. "Hi. I'm the dad," he said, dropping the bag near the foot of the bed. He looked around at the room, and said, "New home, I guess."

It was. But I paid little mind to the stark interior design and never thought once about how the sterile dorm room would be where I would sleep, study, play guitar, and watch my roomie get stoned every morning. Instead, I got right to work. I hung up clothes, plugged in the clock radio, placed books on the shelf. Mom made my bed. Dad fiddled with one of the window cranks, adjusting it with a screwdriver so it closed more tightly. I was settled in less than an hour.

"There you go," my mother said, fluffing a bed pillow. "Do you need anything else?"

In 1974 when Mom asked that question, I assumed she wanted to know if I needed another blanket, a nightlight next to my bed, my socks folded. But years later, after having my own children and watching them search for their own places in the world, I recognized how layered Mom's question really was. *Do you need anything?* My mother wasn't asking about *things*; she was asking whether I needed a hug, a word of encouragement, a reassuring sign that everything so unusual and foreign today would feel good, right, and perfect tomorrow. I was just 18 years old and there I was in this new, strange place. I'd traveled nearly 100 miles from home, the house on Vernon Avenue in Pittsburgh, to be this far away, alone and on my own for the first time. My mother and father never moved out of the neighborhood where they grew up, raising my sister and me in a house on the same street. Distance for my parents, any level of distance, meant goodbyes—tough goodbyes, sad goodbyes. Distance was not about adventure or some wild notion of "seeing the world." No. Distance equaled exit. It meant leaving. Distance meant gone.

My mother certainly knew that if she was going to insist I attend college that it would mean I would move away. But I wonder if she ever considered how it would really happen. If Dad had had his way, I would never have left the neighborhood. I would have finished high school and gone to work in my hometown, using my hands. He was proud of me. I knew that. He wanted me to do what I wanted to do with my life, be who I wanted to be. But it was unmistakable how much my father needed me to stay close, all the time, forever.

More than thirty years after my move to Clarion State, I maneuvered a four-wheeled cart to an elevator of a modern dormitory on the south end of the campus of the University of Missouri. The cart was loaded with cardboard boxes full of CDs and DVDs, a duffel bag of clothes, a large plastic container carrying an alarm clock, a couple bottles of body soap, a big box of Kleenex, and a portable humidifier. Draped over this were more than a dozen shirts on hangers and several folded bath towels. A flurry of students and anxious parents moved in and out of the dorm's glass front door, hauling boxes and luggage and an occasional beanbag chair. It was a hot mid-August day and relief was evident when anyone entered the air-conditioned lobby from the outside. In a corner of the lobby near a collection of overstuffed chairs, an older man and woman, maybe in their early 60s, drank from water bottles, enjoying a break. My respite would come only after several more boxes and elevator trips. But despite what remained, I found the work oddly pleasant, even rewarding, as long as I stayed busy. My son, Casey, the first born, was leaving home, and in the hot midday hours of a Missouri afternoon, I had a job to do.

Being far away from home was not unusual for Casey. In middle school he traveled to Australia, Fiji, and New Zealand with a group of student ambassadors. He had been to the Dominican Republic and Europe on family vacations. And after his high school graduation, he visited Egypt and France on his own, traveling with a tour group for a time and meeting up with friends in Paris. It all sounds rather privileged, a rich kid's experience. Yes, he was fortunate. Rich? No. But, yes, his mother and I had good jobs. Still, it was his innate wanderlust and adventurous soul that fueled Casey's globetrotting, not his parents' determination to shape him or belief that it would somehow be "good for him." His mother and I had not been world travelers by any stretch, growing up in families that believed visiting Niagara Falls or Nags Head, North Carolina was a big deal. Casey, on the other hand, was already embracing the globe at the age of twelve. Travel was deep inside him. It came naturally. One cannot force the love of experience.

We needed the rest of the afternoon to get Casey settled in his dorm room—a rather small space appointed with bunk beds, a pair of desks built into the wall, and a bathroom that would be shared by four students, two in an adjoining room. After he attended dorm orientation in one of the shared living spaces, Casey, his mother, and I went to dinner, I believe it was a hamburger place in Columbia's downtown. We wanted it to be a celebratory supper. His mother and I, I'm certain, finished a bottle of wine, and I'm certain we ordered a couple of deserts to share. Our day had been like many that day—repeated all over Columbia, Missouri many times over—the new student eager yet a little uneasy and mom and dad excited yet nervous, coming together to build a new home and crown a new beginning. We were not unique. Every family faced anticipated separation in its own way, but at the core we were all going through the same thing. And like many, we believed our son would eventually find his way, he would discover a way to connect, fit-in, explore, and flourish. We were not concerned. What we were most worried about was ourselves.

My mother had a phrase she repeated many times over when toddler Casey first began to balance on his own little legs: "When they start to walk, they are no longer walking toward you," she would say, "they are walking away." She knew this well; she knew what direction I was headed when I took my first step. "It's life," she would say. "You give your children the guts to move on and then you let them go."

Marie and I stayed in a local hotel that night. The next day we drove back to the campus to say our goodbyes. Casey embraced his mother and then me on the concrete sidewalk near the front door of his dormitory. All around us other parents and their children performed similar ceremonies—a hug, a kiss, a handshake, a few tears. Casey's goodbye was not burdened with overpowering emotions, at least not on the outside. There was no lingering.

"Okay, okay," I remember him saying. "I probably ought to go."

I remembered all the other times we had separated for those earlier adventures. I remembered how wonderful the trips had been, and I reminded myself I would see him soon.

We all must separate. We all leave those we love. There is no such thing as forever. Life is a series of comings and goings; our children intuitively discover this just as we do. They understand that we must abandon our homes to find our new ones, and leave our hearts behind in hopes that our souls will be endlessly restored.

Marie and I moved together toward the car in the nearby parking lot. She was stiff and rigid, a defense, it seemed, against what was inside.

"He never looked back," she said.

Casey's mother cried heavy tears as we left campus for home, both of us eventually settling into gloomy silence, saying not a single word to each other for six long hours.

The Beauty of Blindness

I was blind. Not unaware or emotionally disconnected. Not
that sort of blindness. Instead, I was without adequate sight, legally blind without being totally blind, and still, I was driving.
It was not a black-of-night kind of blindness, but a degree of
sightlessness, like trying to see through eyeglasses smeared thick
with Vaseline. The sun was setting, the fading light making it
even more difficult to see my way. Traffic was heavy in the last
half of a weekday rush hour, and I had ten miles yet to travel.

When I scheduled Lasik surgery, the doctor was very
clear about what would be the state of my vision in the hours
after the procedure. "You cannot drive," he said. "Get a ride
from someone else," he told me, "and then go to sleep. When
you wake up in the morning, you'll be able to see everything
without corrective lenses of any kind. And remember," he
stressed, "someone else must drive you home."

I drove home anyway. Alone.

There had been an attempt to arrange a ride, but sched-
ules did not match, and it was going to be hours before I could
be transported home. So, my plan was to steal out of the doctor's office when the hour-long surgery was complete. I would
thank the medical receptionist, lie about my ride waiting outside, and make for the exit. I did exactly that and nearly hit my

head on the glass door, seeing it just inches before I would have slammed into it. Once on the sidewalk, I slowed my pace, gingerly and methodically stepping toward where I remembered parking my car.

It was second grade when I began wearing eyeglasses for nearsightedness—first, thick-framed black glasses, then the big-framed tortoise shell style, and finally the round wire rimmed style in high school, like the ones John Lennon had. I don't remember being self-conscious about having to wear corrective lenses, but I do recall how comforting it was to see my favorite teacher in 6th grade, Mr. Madison, wearing the same clunky Buddy Holly-esque frames. He was the kind of teacher who was hard not to like, tossing a football with the boys at recess and letting us play checkers and Monopoly at the end of the day if we'd finished our spelling practices on time. I can still see him leaning on his heavy wooden desk in his worn brown corduroy jacket, black pants, his John Kennedy haircut, and those glasses, telling us in the minutes before the last bell of the school day to remember to take the time to read each night.

In high school I auditioned for a part in the big play. The drama club was producing *The Importance of Being Earnest*, Oscar Wilde's masterpiece. My English teacher, Mrs. Papier, encouraged me to try out. I never would have considered it myself. Strangely, and unexpectedly, I got the role of Lane, the manservant to Algernon, the colorful dandy who loved champagne and was bad with money. I was told to play Lane like a "typical English butler." I remember the director saying those exact words. I had no idea what a "typical butler" was supposed to be like. "And," she said, "lose the glasses." I said my lines in a bad English accent and executed my stage directions in dozens of rehearsals and three performances on the big auditorium stage through fuzzy vision.

I got a few laughs playing Lane. That's all an actor needs. So, I set my sights on several other school productions over the remaining years of high school, even directed a one-act play. It was one the administration wasn't too happy about. The name of it escapes me, but the plot centered on the first school day after the Soviet Union had taken over the United States. These were the years of the Cold War, the Leonid Brezhnev years, and there was one scene where the characters in the play, the students in the classroom, cut up an American flag. It wasn't a real flag. Our teacher wouldn't allow it. Instead it was a representation. We still received plenty of flack from the principal. My parents attended that show and all the shows I was involved in, and after one particular senior production, on the drive home, my mother wondered if I might be considering acting as a career and if I should think about permanently losing my glasses. "They make contact lenses now. We can ask the eye doctor." She thought I might be ready for stardom, a movie career, Broadway, and, in her mind, stars didn't wear glasses. Her favorites were Humphrey Bogart, Cary Grant, and Paul Newman. No spectacles for any of them.

I was fitted for contacts, the hard kind, the only style made in 1973. They were tinted green to enhance my hazel colored eyes. "It will make them look like emeralds," the doctor told me. "The girls will love them," he said. And green they were. Ridiculous green, like the color of a Rolling Rock beer bottle. I'm not sure the girls really loved them, but they certainly were curious enough. Girls I didn't know or would never have talked to stared into my pupils. "Your eyes," they'd ask, "are they really that green?"

In the spring of my senior year—after getting rid of the glasses in the switch to those bright green contacts—I was cast in one of my final high school roles. I played a blind man. I don't remember the character or the play, only that I was to use a blind man's cane and would not wear dark sunglasses. "Not right for this part," the director said. Mrs. Papier, the director of the play, wondered if one could purchase black contacts, the kind that would simulate blindness. I don't believe she ever pursued it, but she was big on authenticity, so in the early rehearsals she had me run my lines and walk through all the stage directions with my eyes closed. I bumped into chairs, knocked over lamps, staggered over my fellow actors, tripped and fell on the stage. In the final rehearsals, I opened my eyes, but had to gaze into the distance. "Like a blind man," she demanded. "Look into nothingness."

I once worked at a radio station with a morning announcer who was slowly losing his eyesight to a degenerative disease. One Saturday we attended a University of Pittsburgh football game together, and the only way he felt comfortable moving through the dim tunnels in the stadium was to hold my arm. We walked slowly up the ramps to our seats. He never panicked. I worried about him, but I didn't need to. Years later, I worked with a blind man, sightless since early childhood. He was an overnight music host at a local radio station. I used to wonder if he could sense the darkness of night or if he relied on others to tell him when the moon was out. "There are benefits to being blind," he joked once. I was coming to work in the morning and he was leaving for home. "No one ever asks you for directions," he said, smiling. I smiled too, but later felt guilty about it. Each early morning, I watched him tap his cane along the hallway floor, through the lobby, and out the door. I never asked him how he got home. Did he walk? Take the bus? How did he know the bus was coming? The sound? But they all sound the same, don't they? How did he know it was his bus? I wondered if he, because of his blindness, had developed a sixth sense. Science has found evidence that the sightless don't only adapt to blindness, their brains actually adjust; the grey matter remakes itself. The part of the brain that helps control the lost sense is repurposed to heighten the other senses. A sort of rewiring takes place, a makeover that the sighted never experience.

So, on the day of the Lasik surgery, even with my severely impaired eyesight, I still believed I could drive myself home without incident. I stepped slowly to my car, searching my coat pocket for the keys. I wanted to move more quickly, believing a nurse in the ophthalmologist's office might soon come chasing after me, but I knew I shouldn't. Rushing would bring attention. I clicked the key fob, heard the beep signaling the doors were open, and slid into the driver's seat. With my hands on the wheel at the 10 and 2 positions, I looked out the windshield and took a heavy breath. *This is not the best idea*, I thought. *But I can do it. I'll take my time. Go the back streets. It's just a few miles.*

The parking lot was easy enough to navigate, but when I reached the traffic light where the lot's exit met the main road, I noticed that the stop-and-go lights appeared nearly the same—colorless, grayish, at best. The red and green lights might as well have been identical. Luckily, there was a car behind me. The driver beeped his horn, twice, so I pressed on the gas pedal and moved cautiously through the intersection. I had mapped out in my head the best route to take—about ten miles, two more stop lights, and five turns in all—to get me safely to my driveway and home.

After the blind role in high school and the coworkers at the radio stations, my encounters with blindness were only occasional. Like many, I sometimes saw a sightless man or woman crossing a city street, clutching a cane or the leash of a guide dog. In one neighborhood where I frequented the corner coffee shop, I watched, through the big picture window, a blind man navigate his way across two busy intersections.

There was nothing remarkable about him, and only because I had been seated at the window and he had directly crossed my path, did I offer him any thought. I'm certain I considered his small journey—the contemplative stops at the street corner, his head tilting back, and his nose raised upward a bit to the sky as if to sense what was before him. This made me think about that old saying: *The blind man seeing more than I am.* I thought about Ray Charles, Stevie Wonder, Jose Feliciano, and Andrea Bocelli. The Italian tenor was born with very poor eyesight and became permanently blind after a football accident when he was 12 years old. There's a gospel group called the Blind Boys of Alabama. Three of the members cannot see. There are dozens of other sightless musicians. Certainly their brains have rewired to intensify the senses of touch and sound. But what if they were painters? Claude Monet painted with failing eyesight, creating his Water Lily series while visually impaired. Van Gogh was rumored to be colorblind. Esref Armagan, a Turkish painter born without eyes, has been painting with oil for years, creating delicate works of muted colors, scenes of rural life and wilderness. He has called his artistic process "painting in the dark."

At one time or another, all of us have considered what it might be like to be blind. We've closed our eyes on the playground and chased our friends. Blind man's bluff. Then there's pin the tail on the donkey and the piñata party game. The blindfold disorients the one with the pin or the stick, and they struggle and stumble. Our friends point fingers and laugh at their inability to navigate. And there's Mr. Magoo from the TV cartoon series, a beloved character in the heyday of animation. The short-statured rich man with the bald head, fedora, and a cheery smile refuses to admit his extreme nearsightedness. However, through every nearly disastrous mishap—moving trains, charging buses, falling trees, brick walls—Mr. Magoo survives. He has uncanny luck, and no matter the danger he encounters and his inability to witness potential peril, everything always works out for him.

Only the last minutes of the day's light remained. Light and dark I could see. Still, I needed my car's headlights. I drove in the right lane of the two-lane roadway, believing that if I got in any real trouble I could pull off easily to a side street or the parking lot of a strip mall. The world beyond the windshield continued to appear gooey; nothing had sharp edges; buildings melted into one another, and the other cars were indistinguishable, appearing only as blobs of matter. I traveled along at just below the speed limit, about 30-miles-an-hour. It was too fast, but I couldn't travel any slower or put on my hazard flashers. That would have attracted the attention of other drivers and maybe the police.

Doing this was wrong. It was dumb. I wasn't just placing *myself* in peril, I was endangering others. My justification for driving blind was highly flawed. I didn't want to be inconvenienced. I didn't want to stay at the eye center for hours, waiting for a ride. I didn't want to leave my car overnight in the parking lot near the doctor's office. I wanted to be home, and blind or not, I was going to get there as soon as possible, get into bed, and sleep until morning when, as the doctor had told me, my sight would be wondrously restored. Misguided determination and impatience produced this foolish strategy, and it was the same combination that would compel me to carry it through, no matter what.

About five miles into the drive, I realized there were fewer cars on the road, and I had begun to adjust somewhat to the blurry world, accepting it and adapting to some degree. But at my final traffic light, as I was about to make a slow, steady left turn to the streets of my neighborhood, a shadow entered my peripheral vision. Another car? A bike? A pedestrian? I snapped my hands tight to the steering wheel, hit the brake, and turned my head. A person—unclear if it was a man or woman, young or old—moved across my windshield. I couldn't hear the words, or see the face or mouth to imagine the expletives being hurled at me, but I could make out wild hand gestures and flailing arms. I'm sure he or she was not waving hello. I blinked my eyes, as if to squeegee away the fuzziness, and raised a hand, palm up, in a gesture of regret.

After nearly hitting someone, I executed the last turns with all-embracing guilt, sighing as I pulled my car into the driveway and turned off the engine. I rested my forehead on the steering wheel and began to cry. The self-imposed anxiety and miles of tension discharged from my pores all at once. I was sweating. My hands trembled. *Jesus*, I thought. *What if I were truly blind?* There had been that possibility, albeit slim. Lasik surgery is not without risk. Astigmatism can be caused by uneven tissue removal, and that could mean even riskier additional surgery. It's rare, I was told, but surgical complications can lead to a permanent loss of vision. *What a stupid thing to consider. I came through the surgery just fine. I am NOT blind. I can see. I am fortunate. I am blessed.* I had no right to speak of blindness or speak *for* the blind. Shame settled in. Not because I drove blind but, instead, because I had been selfish. I misunderstood that my temporary handicap was not the most important thing, my humanity was.

I walked slowly into the house, drank a glass of water, and took a brief shower. I moved the small alarm clock that had been on my nightstand to the dresser on the far side of the bedroom. Pillows were propped; an extra blanket was removed from the foot of the bed. I crawled into the sheets and strained to recognize the distant alarm clock, seeing only distortion. Falling asleep was work—my mind raced and rattled—but when I eventually did, it was a long, hard rest. And in the morning, just as the early sun began to filter through the slightly opened window shades, I lifted my eyelids, and all the way across the room, on top of the dresser, the small digital clock, in backlit white numbers, read 7:06 a.m., crisp and clear.

The Cigarettes of Expatriates

Of all the history, art, and cultural beauty of Paris, the one thing Parisians care most about is the freedom to smoke.

I made my first trip there before France's smoking ban was in place. It's different now. But the legend lingers. The iconic image of the Frenchman dangling a cigarette from his fingertips is still very much a part of the world's view of Paris and the city's café life. Smoking, as restricted as it may now be, is still a meaningful pastime, a symbol of reflection, introspection, and creativity. It remains a badge, in many ways, of the artistic life, of defiance and rebellion.

"It's all I want to do," I said, anticipating my first trip to Paris. "Sit in a café, drink great coffee, wear a beret, maybe, and smoke a cigarette."

People laughed when I said this. *So cliché*, I'm sure they thought. But it was part of my vision of Paris' great society of expatriate artists and writers. It was Hemingway and Fitzgerald. It was Henry Miller. It was John Dos Passos and Ranier Maria Rilke. It was Marcel Proust and James Joyce. Not all were French, of course, but each embraced Paris, the café society, the artist colonies, and although not all of them smoked, they could have and maybe should have. Smoking fit the lifestyle, the milieu, and for me it represented everything about the expatriate, living as an artist in the most creative city in the world.

The trip to Paris was a side journey. The main destination was Scotland to play golf with my father, a gift for my 40th birthday from my then-wife, but she had set up the tour for me to spend some time alone in Paris—to wear that beret, to smoke at a café late into the night. As a joke, she gifted me a black beret and a pack of Dunhills. The cigarettes weren't French but they aptly represented the European smoker. I packed both in my suitcase.

I boarded the Paris Metro from Charles DeGaulle Airport to downtown. I spoke little French, actually three words—merci, bonjour, and oui. I was exactly what Parisians hate—the American who appears not to give a damn about real France and speaks only the language of the despicable Brits. This lack of language skills added to the time spent searching for my little hotel.

After dropping off my luggage and flipping on the hotel room's TV, hoping to catch the weather forecast and, instead, seeing a program featuring bare-breasted women, I hurried out to catch a cab before the sun went down. I stood at the corner and raised my hand as one does in Chicago and New York and watched taxi after taxi zip by me. It took me nearly half-an-hour to discover the cabstand. The sun was setting quickly, so when the taxi pulled up, I searched my mind for the word for "fast" in French. I don't know why I thought I could somehow recall it.

"Arc de Triomphe," I said in my best French accent, twirling my hand in a circle as if the motion was an international symbol for "hurry up." I wanted to see the Arc in the last light of day.

"Oui," the driver said, nodding his head.

We inched our way along the Champs-Elysées in heavy traffic with the last rays of sun glinting off the cab's side view mirror.

"Here," I said. "Drop me here."

The driver pretended not to understand and shrugged his shoulders.

"I'll get out," I said, pretending to open the door. I then showed him my hand. It held many francs. "Take," I said. He pulled over and took what was there.

"Merci," he said.

My knowledge of French currency matched my language skills. I hoped he had been fair.

I ran down the wide sidewalk of the Champs-Elysées, dodging pedestrians. The sun was nearly out of the sky when I reached the Arc, but the large spotlights at its base shone upward, highlighting its majesty. Napoleon's remains had passed through the Arc. Victor Hugo's body was displayed under it. I stood at the roundabout for a long time, watching the people move through the Place de l'Étoile as car headlights invaded the early evening like giant fireflies, and car horns peppered the Paris air. I reached inside my shirt pocket and pulled out the thin box of Dunhills, tugged the cellophane tab, lifted the red and gold lid, and tapped out a cigarette.

"Avez-vous besoin d'une lumière?"

A man with tussled salt and pepper hair and a leather messenger bag strapped across his chest stepped up beside me. He held a stainless steel lighter in his hand.

"Merci," I said. I placed the cigarette in my mouth and leaned into the flame. A puff of smoke filled a small space between my face and his hand.

"Bonne soirée," he said, stepping into the flow of pedestrian traffic across the plaza.

I remained on the sidewalk, inhaled once and again, then blew smoke in an upward angle into the night.

The next day I rose early. Sunday meant mass at No-tre-Dame.

"Emmenez-moi à Notre-Dame, si'l vous plaît," I said to the taxi driver. I had asked the clerk at the hotel before going to the cabstand how to alert the driver to my destination. I practiced those French words several times, but my rookie status remained evident. It was such clunky French; I was surprised he didn't throw me out.

It was 7 a.m., early I thought, but when the driver pulled up near the plaza in front of the cathedral, the crowd was already overflowing. *Maybe they are waiting to get inside for mass,* I thought. But as I moved closer, I could hear a voice over loudspeakers and then a choir. This *was* mass. The inside was packed, and worshippers stood in the plaza, praying and now singing with the choir's young voices. I stood near the rear of the crowd. Bells began to ring.

An elderly woman wearing a blue scarf around her gray hair stood to my right, softly singing from her small hymnal. She noticed me and smiled. The crowd's singing continued, and I began to sway to the holy tones, a Gregorian-like psalm void of meter. The haunting melody pulled me into myself. I was now alone among the masses yet experiencing a kind of communal peace. The woman nodded, acknowledging my acceptance of the shared music. I flashed back to early years in church with my parents. The ritualistic service and the top-down preaching had intimidated me, but I had been able to find something in the mass in which I could connect. *Peace be with you. And also with you.* The ceremonial shaking of hands with those next to you in the pews was the only practice of the mass that was honest. The shared music of Notre-Dame reminded me of that.

"Peace be with you," I whispered to the woman as the crowd's singing subsided.

"Merci, monsieur" she replied.

The faithful slowly dispersed. The bells continued to ring. And if only for a few moments, there were angels.

That night I found myself at the Café de la Paix directly across from the Paris Opera House. At midnight it is no longer a tourist spot. Instead, the cafe returns to the people of Paris, to the neighborhood. I took a small table near the door, just inside the patio. Through the window, I could see the steps to the Opera House. The café's kitchen was still open, and I ordered a glass of Bordeaux and a strawberry crêpe.

The Boulevard des Capucines was quiet except for a young man waiting under a lamplight outside the restaurant across street. He sat on a moped, the engine running, and held a single flower in one hand. From my distance it appeared white, maybe yellow. Every few moments, he would look to the restaurant's door and then back to the boulevard. He waited for many minutes, occasionally revving the scooter's engine as if it might urge along whomever or whatever he was expecting.

I had spent the day with Hemingway's *A Moveable Feast*, taxiing and walking to Les Deux Magots, Shakespeare and Company, near the Seine on The Left Bank, and Harry's New York Bar. Hemingway's celebration of the Parisian life, published after his death, had once been revered in France but had faded from attention. Decades later, *A Moveable Feast* would again be a best seller in Paris. Pride in the city's artistic history after deadly terrorist attacks would elevate Hemingway's memoir to the city's most-read list of books. The French would buy more than five hundred copies a day. But during my time there, Hemingway's Paris had been lost to the ages except for literary geeks. I walked the streets, rested on benches, and sat on bar stools where Hemingway had been, where the Lost Generation was born. My day may have been a cliché to many, a tourist trap, much in the way Pamplona's Running of the Bulls lost its ancient beauty in recent times. Too many fraternity brothers now see it as a bucket list event, a "look-what-I've-done" drinking festival one can boast about. But I did not mind living in a cliché for a few hours. Clichés are born out of authenticity. They come from enduring admiration or the honesty of archetypes. There's truth in clichés. The day's expedition was one about which a true Parisian might roll his eyes, but I liked my clichéd gifts of the beret and the cigarettes I received before the trip, and I was prideful of my day's tour.

Across the boulevard from where I had remained with my wine and dessert, another cliché was unfolding. Out of the restaurant door came a young woman—tall, thin-framed, shoulder length, dark hair. She stopped at the top of the three-step stairs, shook her hair behind her, and tied it in a ponytail. The small knapsack she carried was thrown over her back. The man on the moped handed her the flower, kissed her, and gave her the helmet that had rested on his seat. The woman slid her body on the rear of the moped's seat, secured the helmet, and wrapped her arms around the man's waist. He revved the engine, glanced out toward the street, and sped off along the boulevard, past the Opera House and out of sight.

"Un autre verre de vin, monsieur?" the waiter asked.

I nodded, assuming he was asking if I would keep drinking. "May I take it outside?" I asked.

"Oui," he said, not seeming to mind my English.

There were only a few patrons remaining inside the café— two couples at separate tables on the far side of the room, an older woman sitting alone with a glass of white wine, and a man savoring his coffee. Outside there was no one. The large umbrellas had been lowered, and many of the green cane chairs had been pushed to a corner of the patio. I sat at the table nearest the Opera House and lifted from my jacket the pack of Dunhills. This time I had remembered a lighter.

"Votre vin, monsieur." The waiter placed the glass and a white linen napkin on the table.

"Merci."

I had left the beret at the hotel—too self-conscious to wear it. But I had the Dunhills. The initial drag stung the throat, but when the smoke reached the lungs, it quenched some long, unsatisfied craving. And the Parisian air, crisper earlier in the day, had become dense with the night, like a soft cotton coat draped over a lover's shoulders.

Paco is Dead

Larry was my best friend in those days. Of the handful of college companions in the late 1970s, Larry was the one who stands out. First and foremost, he was funny. He would do just about anything for a laugh, including a silly take on the Robert Palmer song, "Bad Case of Loving You." Larry regularly wore big, clunky hiking boots. I don't remember the brand, but they were an unwieldy style that secured one's foot like an astronaut's moonboot tied with red laces wrapped through big metal grommets. When the Robert Palmer song would come on the radio or out of the speakers of a turntable in an off-campus apartment, Larry would leap up, balance on the large toes of those boots, and sing out his version of the lyrics, "Doctor, doctor, give me the news! I got a bad case of TIP-TOE shoes!" It was so ridiculous, and he did his signature move with such grace and flair, that it was impossible not to laugh. Other friends had wit, surely, but Larry was built for laughter, the kind of humor that was both self-effacing and part of his personal design.

Larry and I had a mutual friend. We called him Paco. I don't remember anyone calling him anything else. That wasn't his real name. He wasn't Hispanic. Probably German or Irish, I'd guess. I don't remember his true first or last names ever being mentioned with any regularity, at least not around our friends. Some of us may have been vaguely aware of his given name, but Paco was just Paco to us. No one was sure how he got the nickname, maybe in high school or in the early college days, but nicknames just kind of happened.

Paco and Larry lived together off campus for a time. There was plenty of dope smoked and cheap beer and bad tequila to be shared. The two of them didn't always get along, if I remember correctly. It might have been something about girl-friends staying too many days at their place, or dishes piling up in the sink, or being late with the cash for the rent.

Many years after college, Larry telephoned me to tell me the news he'd heard from another old friend.

"Paco's dead," Larry said.

It had been twenty-seven years since our time at Clarion State College, a state school in the mountains of central Pennsylvania. Larry lived in Pittsburgh now. I was in Chicago. We did our best, not always successfully, to connect a couple of times a year and catch up.

"Didn't he have cancer?" I asked.

"Yeah, he's dead. Something, huh?" Larry wondered.

"Wow. How did we miss that?"

"All those years. So many people just disappear into the shadows," Larry said.

They say your college friends are your friends for life. That's not necessarily true. I still have friends from college, but the label "friends" may not be quite right anymore. Larry and I talk occasionally, and when I've been back to Pittsburgh to visit, we get together for a beer or dinner, and it's a lot like old times. But that's not true for most of the others in that college group. Facebook has helped to reconnect, but we really do little more than leave a brief comment on a photo of someone's family dog or their kids, or *LIKE* something they've posted about the state of the world. We have not truly re-mained *friends* in the deep-rooted sense. And as for Paco, well, he had never been a Facebook friend.

I met Paco at the college radio station, like many of my other friends, a nearly inseparable group at the time. Almost all of us had dreams of becoming rock-n-roll disc jockeys, and some of us played live music together. I had an acoustic guitar. Paco played bass. Larry occasionally blew the harmonica. My girlfriend sang lead and harmony. Larry's off-and-on girlfriend also played guitar. She taught me how to play Leonard Co-hen's "Suzanne." I taught her Crosby, Stills and Nash's "Help-lessly Hoping." Some of us played together at the local eatery inside the student union on campus, and Paco and I played a few coffeehouses together with another guitarist friend from my high school days. There was a lot of Dylan and Neil Young, but what I remembered most was when Paco started thumping out the bass line to Pink Floyd's "Money" during a short break between songs at one coffeehouse appearance. The crowd im-mediately recognized it. Funny how bass lines can be a song's signature—Lou Reed's "Walk on the Wild Side" or Queen's "Another One Bites the Dust." Paco knew the power of a great bass line. "Listen closely to The Beatles' 'Paperback Writer.' Fabulous. McCartney is a master," he said after listening to vinyl one Friday night at a friend's apartment.

Paco was a comer-and-goer in our group, moving in and out of our circle but always coming back to us. Paco had other groups of friends, guys he'd buy weed from and his Disco bud-dies. Paco loved K.C. and the Sunshine Band. I don't know how he found any of that crap appealing and yet was still able to play the elegant bass line to Dan Fogelberg's "Part of the Plan." I think it had something to do with the underlying sexuality of Disco. His girlfriend loved the god-awful stuff, so if he was going to get some, he had to like Disco. That was my take. He married that girl while they were both still in school, and my girlfriend at the time and I stood up at their wedding at a little Lutheran church, I think it was, just a few blocks from campus.

It was just after my graduation when I lost touch with Paco. He had a year or two to go, if I remember. Larry kept in contact for a time but then there was nothing for years. I had heard somewhere that Paco ended up in Atlanta working at a recording studio. Then there was talk about an illness for a time; someone said it was cancer, but it was never confirmed. Fact is—we didn't really even try to confirm the story.

All of those college friends are now pushing 60 years old— all of us who had once believed we were going to change the world. We missed the tumultuous but electrifying 1960s, graduating in 1978, '79 and '80. We were in middle school and younger when Martin Luther King Jr. was assassinated, when Robert Kennedy was shot in the head, when cities burned and campuses erupted. The Kent State shootings happened when we were freshmen in high school. The Vietnam War ended when we were high school seniors, some of us younger than that.

"Don't you want something meaningful to protest, like the students did back then?" I asked Larry once on a drunken and weed-infused night.

Larry raised his fist in the air like the black athletes at the Olympics in 1968 and blurted, "Power to the people!" The gesture and comment were both serious and sarcastic. It was easy to think we would have been part of the demonstrations that rocked the country, but I wondered if we would have simply stayed on the sidelines, like most college students.

Paco saw it differently. He laughed at my question and Larry's fist, and asked, "Seriously guys. Isn't it better to live in the present than the past?" He was our Zen master, without even trying, without even knowing.

Sometime later in the semester, Larry and I and our respective girlfriends set off on a road trip to Cedar Point, a big amusement park near Toledo. It was about a four-hour drive from campus, and to get there, one had to travel the highway just outside the campus of Kent State. We all agreed to stop and "see where the kids were shot." It was an eerie visit, an awkward drive through campus asking students some six years after the shootings where we might find the school's Commons. "Those kids were us," my girlfriend said, walking from where we had parked the car to the spot where the body of Jeffrey Miller once laid, the dead student in the Pulitzer Prize winning photograph.

All of us were silent for a long time on the drive from Kent State to Cedar Point until I wondered, "Isn't that Paco's name?"

The three others thought for a moment.

"The dead kid?" Larry asked.

"Paco's name is...ah...Jeff? Isn't it?" my girlfriend wondered.

"I have no idea," Larry's girlfriend said.

"Martin," Larry said. "It's Jeff *Martin*. Jeffery Martin. He writes it on his checks. And I had a class with him last semester. The prof wasn't going to call him Paco."

"Jeff Martin might as well have been Jeff Miller," I said.

A few days after the trip, I saw Paco outside the campus cafeteria hall.

"How was the road trip?" he asked.

"We stopped at Kent State," I said.

"Where?"

"Kent State."

"You know someone who goes there?"

"No. Wanted to see where the students were shot."

"Kids shot?" he asked.

"You don't know about Kent State?" I was distressed.

"Wait," he said, with minor recognition. "The song 'Ohio.' CSN&Y. 'Tin soldiers and Nixon coming.'"

I nodded. "We saw the spot where one student was killed."

"We played the song at one of the coffeehouse gigs," Paco recalled.

"We did."

"Fucked up, man," Paco said. Then his mind quickly turned. "You going in to get something to eat? I'm starving."

Paco didn't see the incident at Kent State as I did, and I was upset he hadn't put it in the perspective I thought it deserved or hadn't considered, as my girlfriend had, that any of those students could have been one of us, our group, our friends. My relationship with Paco changed on that day. I realized we were different people who just happened to cross paths through radio and music. We remained friends, but things had changed. Still, decades later, as I talked about his death with Larry, deep sadness came over me.

"It doesn't feel right. I should have known about Paco dying," I said.

"Long time ago," Larry said, trying to justify the detachment.

"But he was one of us," I said.

There was silence on both ends of the phone.

Before hanging up, Larry and I pledged not to allow so much time to pass before speaking again. We pledged to get together someday soon, visit in our respective cities, but we knew it would be less than likely. And we promised to try to keep in better touch with those old friends, but we both knew that, too, was doubtful.

Some weeks later, Larry telephoned again.

"Are you ready for this?" he asked, excitedly.

"You're going to be grandfather?" I joked.

"Paco?"

"Yeah?"

"He's alive."

"What!?"

"Paco is *not* dead," Larry laughed. "We had the fucker dead."

"But what about the cancer?"

"Survived it. He's fucking alive!"

Larry must be wrong, I thought. I was just getting used to Paco's death.

"I talked to him," Larry added.

"What the hell?"

"He called me. Out of the blue."

"I feel cheated," I said, sarcastically. "I fucking grieved."

"Bastard," Larry said. "He got a kick out of the story, though, all of us thinking he was dead."

Paco was still in the Atlanta area, where he had first traveled after college. He was in the music industry, as he'd been for years, selling something or another related to studio work. Larry said he wasn't really sure what he did, couldn't remember exactly what Paco had told him. But it didn't matter. "He's fucking alive," Larry said again. "The guy is alive."

Larry and I talked about old times with Paco, brought up a few other names from that group of ours, and wondered where they were living, what they were doing, if any really *were* dead. We were like the old men at a veteran's hall. I missed the military draft. It was abolished just before I turned eighteen and went off to Clarion State. I never had the "brotherhood" of Army life, the kind of experience my father insisted bonded him to other men like nothing had or ever would again. My brotherhood came in another way.

Minutes after hanging up with Larry, I considered calling him right back. *I should get Paco's phone number*, I thought.

I should reach out to him. But I didn't. Still, I couldn't help recall what Paco had said that night in his apartment so many years ago: *It's better to live in the present than the past.* In that new moment, in that here and now, Paco was no longer the guy who was once so ignorant of Kent State, no longer the guy who loved shitty Disco music. Instead, Paco was the old, albeit nearly forgotten, friend who once had given us advice we all would be better off heeding. I'm certain we didn't think much of what he said at the time he said it. In the realm of significant thought, what Paco said was entirely minor in scope, far from profound philosophy. However, it was said at the right time and the right place, when all of us in that group of college friends were discovering how we fit in the big world, who we were, and why any of it was important. Paco's words, words from a friend, simple and offhanded as they may have seemed at the time, can be unwittingly profound. They stick. Those words, like the old friends who are forever tethered to us, linger in the subconscious and remain imprinted on the heart.

Forever Memphis

Graceland was gloomy. It was rundown and tired. The tour guide at Elvis' mansion on a Memphis hill said it had been left just as it was when the singer died. There was a tear in the fabric on the pool table and the guide said it happened during a party not long before his death. "Someone got a little aggressive," he said. "It was never repaired." Elvis died in 1977. The trip my son and I took to Memphis was in 2004.

Graceland is now considered a museum, but it isn't really. It's a home, a place left set in the past. Abandoned. It was grand when Elvis bought it in 1957. It is no longer so grand. The more than thirteen acres where the house sits was named after the daughter of the previous owner, Stephen C. Toof, founder of S.C. Toof & Co., a respected printing firm in Memphis. Her name was Grace. Elvis loved the name.

Graham and I had been talking about taking a trip together, just the two of us.

"How about Memphis?" I asked.

"What's there?" Graham was twelve years old.

"Sun Records, Beale Street, the Blues Highway."

He tilted his head.

"All musical history," I explained. "You know that Dylan song I play in the car?"

Graham laughed. I played a lot of Dylan songs in the car.
"'Highway 61 Revisited,'" I said.

Graham nodded with some recognition.

"The road runs from New Orleans to Minnesota, Dylan's home state. But the section from St. Louis south is known as the Blues Highway."

"And Sun Records?" Graham asked.

"Sun Studio. Where Elvis played. Johnny Cash recorded. We can go inside," I said. "And Beale Street is where all the bars are. Blues in the air, you might say."

"Will we drive?" Graham asked.

"Road trip," I said, "and we can go inside Graceland if you want."

Standing with others at the entrance before beginning the tour of Elvis' home, where large musical notes and the images of guitarists are wired into the gate, Graham wondered, "Does anyone still live here?"

"Not anymore," I said.

"Then why do they still call it his home?"

I thought for a moment. "Well, it *was* a home."

Graham peered through the gate. "It seems sad."

That night we walked Beale Street. Music soared from the bars and onto the sidewalks. Because Graham was just a kid, we couldn't go inside anywhere to hear the music, but the March air was warm enough for the bars to prop open their doors to the night and let the songs come out, mixing the cries of electric guitars with the spark of neon lights. Electrified sounds and brightly glowing glass tubes go together on Beale Street.

I peeked through the window of one of the taverns.

"All the good ones sweat," I said.

A tall, thin man stood on a dimly lit stage, crouching and leaning forward and backward, his guitar tight against his belt buckle. Blue stage lights caught heavy perspiration on his forehead.

Graham was now standing beside me.

"Drummers are the ones who sweat," he said.

Graham had been teaching himself the drums, took a few lessons, but did better learning on his own, pounding away on the drum set in his mother's basement until he got it right.

On one side of the street was a used record shop. I don't remember the name. LPs were stacked from floor to ceiling, in corners, on chairs, in racks. Along the top shelf, next to the ceiling, sat several pieces of memorabilia, including a couple of guitars, their bodies signed with Sharpies by the artists who once played them—Slash, John Mellencamp. There were also several signed record albums.

"I see the first Led Zeppelin up there," I said.

"Jimmy Page and Robert Plant came in the place," the clerk said. "They were shopping, looking around. I knew who they were, but I let them do their thing."

"Were they playing nearby?" I asked.

"That night. It was like two in the afternoon."

"So they signed the record?"

"They came up to the desk to buy something, can't remember what, and I just asked them. They were great."

"How much?"

"The owner says he wants $1000 for the record now. But I don't really think it's for sale, to tell you the truth."

Graham and I bought a couple small items from the store, souvenirs. I can't recall what. Out on the sidewalk, Graham said, "I know why Elvis loved this place." He looked around and said, "Music is everywhere."

We found a small barbeque place on the other side of town. On the wall at each booth was the work of a local artist. The waitress said the painter was a teacher at a college nearby.

"These for sale?" I asked.

"Ah, I don't think so," the waitress said. It was clear she had never been asked the question.

"I'd love to buy it."

"Well, I can ask."

I felt somewhat pretentious pursuing this, like a rich man reminding a potential seller that everyone has a price.

It was a 2x2 painting, folk art style, and it depicted Highway 61. Along the road were images of Robert Johnson, B.B. King, Bob Dylan. Guitars lined the pavement, the colors vibrant and animated.

"Don't you love this?" I asked Graham.

"Dad, what if she says he wants $500?"

"I'm struck by it," I said, ignoring the potential cost.

Graham ordered a Pepsi. I got a beer. The waitress said she was trying to reach the manager on the phone. We ate barbeque pork sandwiches and waited.

Graham and I had been in Memphis for almost two full days. We heard the music and found it easy to melt into the South, so much of it welcoming without ever saying so. Memphis puts an arm around you and promises to make you feel at home. It celebrates its past but also promises a future. There's heat in Memphis, even in the early spring. It's not the heat of climate, not of weather and sunlight, but of pride and passion, of steadfastness and honesty. The Civil War is here. God is here. Johnny Cash is here, his aura—big and gutsy. The Negro is here, so is the Black man, and the African American. Martin Luther King Jr. was assassinated here. Johnny Ace was buried here. Aretha Franklin was born here. Jack Daniels is here. The Mississippi River is here. The purple iris is here. The tulip poplar is here. Memphis is grace. Memphis is sweet tea. Memphis is home.

"He doesn't want to sell it," the waitress said, "but we do have the artist's name. Maybe he can paint something for you." She handed me a slip of paper with a handwritten phone number.

I thanked her. We finished our barbeque and called it a night.

Sun Studio is a strangely shaped brick building. It comes to-gether at one end near the corner of Union and Marshall in downtown Memphis; a big hollow-body electric hangs above the front door. Inside it feels like an old record shop, dusty without actually being dusty. A middle-aged woman was at the front counter. She smiled and offered the prices for the museum and a tour. Photographs were everywhere and records for sale. Buttons. Guitar picks. It was a small place. One some-times imagines historical places as physically big. Nearly always they are not.

After pointing out the souvenirs, small gifts, and plaques throughout the entrance, the woman walked us down a short hallway to the holy space, the control room and the small studio. To the left of the booth was a large black-and-white photo of the original fabulous four: Presley, Perkins, Lewis, and Cash. Just down from that hung an enormous photo of Elvis—a young handsome man, sweating, holding a micro-phone, singing. Several guitars sat on their stands. A stand-up acoustic bass leaned against the wall near the door. A small piano, floor amps, and an old reel-to-reel machine were on the opposite side. Part of Sun is a museum, but not this part. This is a workspace.

The woman pointed to a corner of the studio where a chrome microphone stand rose from its metal base, a bulky 1950s Shure model on top. On the floor below were two swatches of black tape forming an X.

"When Bob Dylan was here the first time, he knelt down and kissed that spot," the woman said.

Elvis stood there. Sang there. Shook it there.

"This was the beginning," she said. "Memphis was his home and Sun was his soul because it all started right there. On that X."

Graham and I put our arms over one another's shoulders and stood before the microphone. We smiled, and the woman took a photograph.

For the next hour, we studied the photos on the walls, admiring the musical instruments, pretending we might be on a break from a day of recording our own music. The woman repeated the names of some of those who had come to lay down tracks. Bono, Bonnie Raitt, and Ringo Starr recorded here. John Mellencamp finished an album at Sun. B.B. King, Howlin' Wolf, and Junior Parker introduced Sun to the Blues in the early 1950s.

Graham didn't know some of those artists, not yet. He'd soon pack his iPod with the heavy metal of Slayer, Slipknot, and Metallica but there would also be Dylan's "The Man in Me," Credence's "Born on the Bayou," Hendrix, Zeppelin, and even some Sinatra. Elvis may not have been on the playlist, but much of what was there had the spirit of Elvis all over it. In the years ahead, we would play songs from our iPhones in the car, just the first few notes, and challenge each other to guess them—my favorites, his favorites, old songs, obscure songs, new songs. I'd play The Beatles and ask, "Who wrote this? Lennon or McCartney?" Graham was a quick study. I did the same with his older brother, Casey. *I'm winning Name*

That Tune in the van ride, he texted me once on his way out west with a group of University of Missouri students, *and I blame you.* A younger Casey played the saxophone for a time, blowing out a pretty good rendition of the song "Tequila" by The Champs. And Graham stayed with the drums, blasting through rock-n-roll in the fierce, self-taught John Bonham style—hard, fast, and sweaty. In time, Graham and I would play together in his basement—he on the drums, me on electric guitar—the two of us prolonging the end of a session with a slamming and frenetic, feedback-fueled rock-n-roll finish—loud and furious. I'd slash and he'd bang until our arms could no longer bear the intensity. I'd pretend to smash my guitar like Pete Townsend and he'd toss his sticks in the air like Keith Moon. We'd laugh in release.

Graham is 24-years old now. His drums sit silent more often than not these days, and my electric guitar—quiet and out of tune—leans silently against the small amp near the wall. Playing together is rare now. Life takes over too frequently. But years ago, inside a legendary studio in Memphis, a father and son began watering fertile musical ground that had once yielded fruit.

The seven-hour drive home to Chicago started in the last light of the late afternoon. We decided we would break for some dinner about halfway, maybe somewhere near Centralia, Illinois. Heading north out of Memphis through a corner of Arkansas on I-55 just north of Burdette, we had begun to settle in with the rhythm of the ride when Graham spotted a road sign.

"Isn't that the Blues Highway?" he asked.

The green sign read: *Blytheville 5-Miles,* and beside it was the highway symbol for *Route-61.*

I nodded.

"Why aren't we on it?" Graham asked.

"It's not really the fastest way. The route runs sort of northwest near the Mississippi River. We want to be more east."

"So what," he said. "It's the Blues Highway."

"It is, but it'll add hours to the trip."

"Dad, when are we ever again going to drive on Highway 61?"

Darkness was quickly moving in. I was already tired, and we had a long way to go. It would likely be after midnight before we'd make it home. I read the next highway sign.

Route 61 to Blytheville 2-Miles.

"Can you reach over the seat and open the guitar case?" I asked.

I had been in the habit since college of bringing my old Yamaha acoustic along with me on trips, especially road trips. For this weekend, the extra baggage seemed a necessity.

Graham stretched over the neck rest, his knee on the middle console, and unsnapped the clasps on the case. He lifted out the guitar, slid his body back into the passenger seat, and cradled the six-string.

"Where's the camera?" I asked.

Graham reached for the small luggage bag we had placed on the front floor and pulled it out.

I took the exit for Blytheville and followed it to the fork in the road less than a hundred yards off I-55. I turned left, and up ahead on the right side was one of those familiar black-and-white road signs you see all across America. *North Route 61.* I heard wheels on gravel as I pulled the car to the shoulder.

"Give me the guitar, and you bring the camera," I said, grabbing the instrument by its neck.

With the car's headlights illuminating the road sign, I held the guitar's body up above my head so that it was directly beside the highway sign, the light reflecting off the sign and the metal strings, a portrait of the highway and an old six-string framed by the black Arkansas night.

Graham backed up and to one side, to be certain not to block the car's headlights, and clicked the camera. I switched the guitar to my other hand and maneuvered it closer to the sign for a different composition. Graham snapped another photo and another. And when we were through, we returned to the car, and I drove back to the road, heading north on Highway 61 for as a long as it would let me.

Guitar Heroes

John came late on a sticky afternoon to the house I had moved into for the summer to invite me to the park in town, the one with the gazebo in the middle, to play guitar with his buddies.

"We've all been strumming it for a long time; some guys are better than others. It doesn't matter, though. We just make noise," John said. "But guitars are always chick magnets, right? So we play." He laughed.

For over ten years, these same five guys tried to get together most every week to jam.

In the spring, my teaching duties at the college in Chicago had wrapped up, and within two days I packed up the Jeep with a duffle bag of clothes, a dozen books, my laptop, a manila envelope with a 300-page manuscript heavily marked with badly needed edits, and my Yamaha acoustic, and headed to College Park, Florida. It took me two days of nearly continuous driving. My home for the summer would be the former home of Jack Kerouac. The Jack Kerouac Project, a foundation that had preserved the old wooden cottage and allowed writers to work and live there, had offered me the place to write for three months. It was a holy space, soon to become a National Historic Landmark, a modest house built in the 1920s, and it sat unassumingly on a quiet street, a massive live oak tree guarding the front yard, its branches scraping the tin roof when the wind blew during late afternoon rainstorms. When I told a friend about that, she said it must have sounded like the pencils of the writing gods scratching out beautiful words. One of the former writer's at the house wrote something similar about tree branches on the roof, I was told. Sometimes at night, I'd stare at the ceiling from the simple twin bed at the far south room of the house and wonder what stories the gods, or Jack, were telling. Kerouac only lived in the house with his mother for a short time in the late 1950s, but it was a significant time for him. He had just released *On the Road* and had been thrown in the caldron of fame. And in the room in the back with the view of the orange tree, he'd typed the final manuscript of *The Dharma Bums*. It was said that an old woman who had lived in the neighborhood for decades insisted she remembered hearing the late night snap of typewriter keys, traveling from the home's rear window.

A week after settling in, the Project asked me to give a reading at a local coffee shop. The little café was one of those cluttered Bohemian places where all the male baristas wore ponytails, and the females sported nose rings. One of them was a painter, and when he'd make my skim latté, he'd create incredible images using the milk's white foam as his paint. One time he crafted a beach scene, complete with ocean waves, a seagull, and the sun. When I wasn't writing at Kerouac's place, this shop became my hangout. I'd find a table in the corner near the window where I could write and read, and chat it up with the regulars. I got to know some of them pretty well; we even exchanged some favorite books. I also left a book or two in the café's tiny sharing library. The little stack of free books fit the place, a shop that did not display prices for its coffee but, instead, asked for donations. "It's up to you," they would say. "Whatever you think we are worth." Some of the money went to a local sports program for middle school students in the neighborhood, some dollars helped a literacy campaign for kids. The café was also the home of a local community theater, a group that performed plays in the rear section of the building in front of as many as thirty patrons sitting in folding chairs. The donated money helped offset the cost of promotion and marketing. People paid well for their coffee.

On the night of my reading, John, the guitar player who would later come to my door, was in the crowd. Afterward, while we sipped coffee, some white wine, and nibbled on oatmeal cookies someone had brought on paper plates, he asked if I had planned to do much else while I was in town. I told him I would probably venture out for some drives—maybe to the ocean a few times—and play the guitar a bit as a way to break up the writing routine. All I had to do was say "guitar" and I was John's best friend. He had six acoustics, if I remember correctly. His favorite was a '60s vintage Martin. He thought Gram Parsons was a genius and Stephen Stills was a highly underrated player. "We should play sometime," he said. A few weeks later he was on the front porch of Kerouac's old home.

All five guys were already at the gazebo when I arrived. It had rained earlier; the grass was soaked, and some of the wooden seats were wet, so they all sat under the roof to one side where it was dry. Two of them had their guitars out; one was already playing.

"There he is," John said as I walked up the walkway to the gazebo. "Get any tail on the way over?" he asked, an extension of the earlier comment he made at my door about how guitars get girls.

"Always worked for me," said Ted, the owner of what looked like a new Taylor.

"The great pussy magnet," said Joe, pulling a twelve-string from its case.

"Looks like you're working on a threesome," I said, trying to make a joke.

It seemed the talk about women and sex was standard procedure for this group—old school, guys being guys. It was somehow ceremonial. I never viewed it as demeaning. But I wonder what their girlfriends or wives would have said.

"How come there are no hotties out here now?" I asked, questioning the difference between the claim and the reality.

"We're fucking old," laughed John. "Marc keeps Viagra in his guitar case."

"Fuck you," Marc said, his eyes remaining on the guitar frets as he worked his way through a simple three-chord progression. Marc was one of a trio who still had his hair, wearing it the same way he did decades ago—parted in the middle, hanging over his ears and the back of the neck. But now the hair was almost entirely gray. Along with John, Ted, and Marc were Tim and Lou, each in his late fifties or early sixties. Two guys wore shorts, three in jeans. One had on a black Canned Heat t-shirt; the other sported a wrinkled navy blue golf shirt with the tail hanging out. Lou's head was shaven. Tim was bald, but he kept it long on the sides, like David Crosby, and wore a bushy salt and pepper goatee. Ted had a full white beard. John was a banker, divorced. Ted and Marc worked together at an insurance company; Ted was Marc's boss. Lou was a retired mailman with two grown kids and two ex-wives. Tim was in sales of some type, hoping to pack it in soon if the economy ever got its act together. He lived with his girlfriend.

"Down here to write. Teach college. Two kids," I said.

"Wife?" Tim asked.

"Nope. Divorced. Six years. We're friends."

"No one is friends with their ex," said Lou, strumming a little more intensely on a minor bar chord.

"I'm lucky."

"Friends with benefits," said John, smiling.

"Jesus, you guys need to get laid," I said.

When I was a teenager, my father never sat me down for that man-to-man talk about girls and sex. Closest he got was an accusatory glare after catching me looking through his *Playboys*. I would guess most men my age, the age of the old hippie guitar players in the park, never had any kind of *real* conversation with their fathers about sex. Maybe some dad gave his kid a condom on a Saturday night and told him not to "knock anyone up," but that was the extent of it. I was never really sure what "the talk" should have been. Certainly words like responsibility would have been part of it, discussions about respect, caring, and love. But that's the storybook ideal, the textbook answer, the words of some child psychologist on how a father should talk to his son about feelings, girls, and sex.

Most of us heard it from our buddies, not from our dads, albeit mostly bullshit. When I was in college and used to jam with a couple of friends from my dorm, one of them once said that playing music, playing the guitar and playing it well, was like good sex, like making love when it's done right. He was probably high. But then some years later I remembered hearing about a study that found the brain released dopamine when you heard or played music, the same way it does when you're making love. And from that moment on, the guitar became my vehicle, a young man's ride into the world of women.

Ted pulled out a couple of joints. "Feel free to take a hit," he said.

"We'll see how the night goes," I said, trying to be polite.

"Cops never suspect a bunch of old guys smoking some pot out here," Ted laughed as he lit up, exhaled blue smoke, and handed the joint to John.

"I think Tim's got some new song he wants to give a whirl tonight," John said. "Right?"

"Let's warm up a bit first," said Lou, chording his way through a G-C-D progression.

"It's an easy thing we always do," he said, quickly getting me up to speed on the routine. "Just follow along."

The sound of six guitars echoed inside the gazebo; the setting was a natural amplifier. After a few rounds through the country-bluegrass progression, Marc broke into a series of riffs, a lead part he had performed a million times. He played flawlessly. "Marc's good," said John. For over an hour we played The Beatles, Dylan, Simon and Garfunkel, and even a Richie Havens tune. Most of it was stuff from our younger days, but we also stumbled our way through some songs by the Wallflowers and something from Ray LaMontagne, everyone hunching over sheets of printed music from guitar tablature websites.

As good as these guys could play together, none of them was a singer, at least not anymore. Smoke and drink and age had limited any range there once may have been. But that didn't appear to matter. They choked out the lines and sang with guts, whining through the words they had belted out hundreds of times before, grinning at people walking through the park, to neighbors who smiled and waved, acknowledging that all must be right with the world if the old guys are doing their thing under the gazebo on a summer night in College Park, Florida.

Nearly two hours passed, the music going silent just long enough for one of us to re-tune or sip from a soda can. And at the end of the evening, as the light softened, our callused fingertips burned, and we were pleased and emboldened, like a marathoner at the finish line.

"Think you guys will ever stop doing this?" I asked as we packed up sheets of music, put away picks, slipped guitars into cases.

"You kidding?" John said. "And give up the rock-n-roll life? The drugs . . . the chicks?"

"Oh yeah," I said. "That would never do."

Playing at the gazebo never became a regular thing. And I learned it wasn't always a regular thing for the guys. Family vacations, doctor appointments, dinners with wives and girl-friends interrupted the schedule. But when they did get to-gether, it was all about the music, the songs, and the guitars, playing until hands cramped, fingers hurt, and hearts emptied.

I left town and the Kerouac house just before Labor Day. I was able to finish the rewrite of my manuscript. But in the days after returning to Chicago, there were many nights when I was unable to find the energy to write, conjure up some-thing meaningful to put on paper. It seemed my creative life had been left behind in Florida. Three months in the thick southern air were hard to rinse away in the gusty weather of a Chicago autumn. Not that I wanted to, it was only that I believed I somehow needed to. I was back in Chicago, and Florida was over, behind me. I had to stop at the dry cleaners, pick up milk, buy new tires for the car, get back to teaching. Certainly, living like a poet in Kerouac's humble home and playing music in the park had been stamped on me for good, but the experience was no longer my day-to-day. How could it be? One familiarity was not the other—different places, dif-ferent tempos. The sun came up over changed horizons.

One night in early November, with Florida several weeks behind me, I lifted my guitar from its case for the first time since my final night in Kerouac's house. I sat in a kitchen chair, placed the guitar on my knee, and strummed my way through the chords to "Mrs. Robinson," The Beatles' "Rocky Rac-coon," worked at learning to play Gram Parson's "Blue Eyes," and thought of those guys in the park, those guitar heroes, and wondered if the powerful magnetic force of a man with a six-string might somewhere be doing its magic. It was then that I recognized the permanence of my time in College Park, the forever mark of my summer. Thrown over my shoulder were satchels of experience, newly acquired belongings of which I was unaware until they had the chance to gather dust. Like recognizing beauty, I missed seeing it until I saw it again, in my mind's eyes, ignited by the music I played in my kitchen. The words I could not write in Chicago, the ones I longed and wrestled to find, had been elusive. The stimulus of that summer, as subtle and peaceful as expected and at the same time unforeseen as it may have been, had faded. I was impoverished. But then there was the music and the memory of six-strings in the park. It was a souvenir I had transported home. It had been nearly two months, and I had yet to unpack the treasures of Florida, believing my days there were somehow separated from all else, unknowingly digging a moat between two places, two spaces. Not only was Chicago part of me, but so was Florida, Kerouac's house, that great coffee café, and the guitars. My time there was not a vacation to Disneyland with the kids, a getaway, to shatter the monotony of routine. I didn't travel to Florida to spend time *away* from life; I took my life with me. I planted some of my soul under that big live oak in Kerouac's yard and under the roof of the gazebo in the park where acoustic music hung in the framing of its ceiling. And in turn, I carried so much else back with me. College Park, Florida was not an isolated outpost of life; it *was* life. I would now live in both places, Chicago and Florida. I would live in all places.

Navajo Nation

There's a road that spills out of the Grand Canyon, not far from the famous lodge on the east side of the park. It serpentines down a hill and lands in a wide open space, arid ground below a broad sky that appears untouchable, distant but yet close, a sky that falls on you before an expansive valley, empty of trees, caressed by blood-colored rocks, forever enveloping endlessness. If God exists, this is where you would find him.

I pulled the RV off the road next to a bluff and stepped out, along with my passengers, a trio who'd traveled beside me for over three thousand miles. It would be five thousand before we'd rest with our journey behind us.

"I have never," I whispered, the way one would in a temple.

My teenage son, Casey, began taking photographs. Graham, his younger brother, stepped to the edge of the rocks to lean in. My friend, Brad, sunglasses pushed back on his head for an unobstructed view, was silent, as if nothing he could say would matter.

The Navajo Nation is more than twenty-seven thousand square miles and it appeared every acre of it, every inch stretched out before us. It was ancient, teaming with echoes. It was as if I had stepped into a primal cathedral, and somewhere

out there angels were watching me, their eyes on all of my religious and spiritual baggage, the trunk loads of guilt, doubt,
and faithlessness.

The church I attended as a kid was a characterless yellow brick
building with a high, modern steeple above the entranceway.
Without the steeple, St. Albert's could have been an insurance
company. There was nothing grand about it. It was a square
box with steel front doors. Inside, it smelled of incense and
mold, the interior just as stark and unforgettable as the outside. The altar was sparse; a large golden challis rested in the
middle of a simple stone table. Behind it, hanging from the
low ceiling, was a large cross, a wooden Jesus nailed to it, red
paint signifying his bloodied hands and feet, a crown of thorns.
Father Hannon ruled the place. He was a stick of a man, tall
and gaunt with salt and pepper hair and a pockmarked face
that had one expression—a scowl. He smelled of Lucky Strikes.

On Sunday mornings I sat with my mother, father,
grandmother, and great aunt and tried to shrink into the dark
wooden pews. I pretended to follow along in the mass book
and sing the words of medieval songs tucked inside worn black
leather hymnals, hoping Father Hannon would never notice
me. He was the one who knew all my sins. He was the one
who knew I had lied to my grandmother about taking the open
pack of Clove gum from her purse. He knew I had thrown that
snowball at the car traveling down our street on a dark January
night. He knew I wanted to kiss the flaxen-haired girl who sat
at the desk in front of me in my elementary school classroom.

On confirmation day, at the age of twelve, we stood in
two lines—the boys in their Sunday suits and ties, and the girls
in frilly dresses and bows in their hair—outside the walnut

confession booths in the rear of the church. One line was for the new young priest and the other for Father Hannon. We were allowed to choose. But when the line for the new priest grew twice the size of Father Hannon's and began to snake far down the aisle along the big stained-glass windows of the saints, my mother insisted I stand in the other line. She wanted me to show Father Hannon some respect.

I sat with my hands in prayer inside the shadowy confessional booth and waited. My little sport jacket buttoned tight around me, my skin hot and sweaty. I had to pee. The silence inside the darkness seemed permanent. I heard the squeak of wood on wood as the small sliding window opened, and in came a slice of dusty, ghostly light. On the other side of the remaining metal screen was Father Hannon. I could hear him breathe.

"Son," he said.

"Bless me, Father, for I have sinned," I whispered.

I don't remember what I confessed, but I'm certain I said nothing about the blonde girl. And I'm not sure what he offered as penance but it was likely some countless combination of Hail Marys and Our Fathers.

A few years later, my father and mother stopped attending church. My grandmother had died after a long illness and because she had not been making regular donations on Sunday mornings, Father Hannon questioned her allegiance to God and the Catholic Church. He refused to offer a funeral mass. After more than a week of debate and arguments, Father Hannon eventually agreed to hold a mass for my grandmother. It was the last time on any regular basis that my parents could be found inside St. Albert's Church. I, however, returned for evening religious classes once a week with the rest of the Catholic boys and girls who went to the public school, and somehow passed the mandatory exam on the saints and the tests on all the sins one could possibly commit.

Twenty years later I was back inside a grand cathedral in Erie, Pennsylvania to be married. But before that I was required to attend regular church-sponsored marriage classes.

"But that's what faith is," the religious counselor said. "You must learn to trust."

"And why would I do that?" I asked. "What proof do I have?"

He asked me what I did for a living.

"Journalist," I said.

"That explains it."

I came back to the church years later when my sons were born. There was no epiphany. I simply acquiesced, agreeing with my wife that it would be best to give the boys some religious upbringing, some foundation they could later build on or reject. As for me, I never voluntarily returned to a Catholic church. And when their mother and I divorced, I did not consider an annulment. What would have been the point?

My religious life had always been fractured. I didn't know what I wanted out of spirituality or why I wanted it. After the divorce, I tried a Lutheran service. It felt too Catholic. I studied Unitarianism for a time and attended a Unitarian church off and on. Sunday services were laced with quotes from Thoreau and Emerson. I thought this might be my spiritual center, but for whatever reason, its lure did not last. I read books on Buddhism and thought I might find the Zen in Zen. But like a young boy jumping from one summer sports camp to another, I failed to master any one thing. What I certainly was doing, however, was searching. That was the singular constant. But whatever it was I was attempting to find, remained helplessly out of reach. I believed in nothing, and at the same time I believed in everything.

With all of this religious baggage, I had found myself on the barren ground of the Navajo Nation.

A summer shower fell from high broken clouds of buffed chrome, and white, filtered rays of sun touched our shoulders.

"Let's take the road awhile," I said.

We climbed back in the RV and drove slowly with the windshield wipers on the intermittent setting. The road before us narrowed and toppled through the valley. For several miles there were no other vehicles and no other sounds but the chug of the RV's engine and a persistent warm wind. To our left was a cabin built from stone and wood, a getaway of four or five small rooms. A man and a woman dressed in jeans and dark colored t-shirts sat on rough-hewn Adirondack chairs in the rust colored dirt near the entrance and watched the sky. They held hands. The woman waved to us and the man pointed to the distance.

A rainbow.

The ribbon had formed across the sky from a plateau to the low mountains. Light rain spritzed the RV windows as we pulled off to the shoulder. Free roaming cattle stood near the edge in the sparse vegetation along the road, ignoring our vehicle and unaware of our presence as we stepped out of the RV to a position on raised ground about twenty-five feet from the road's edge. The rain shower ceased, and the rainbow intensified, the colors becoming deeper and more distinct. My son, Casey, again, took photographs. Graham stood silent under nature's prism, his eyes turned upward.

"How'd we get so lucky?" Brad said, nodding toward the southern sky.

Materializing slowly near the horizon, just above a gathering of slate gray clouds, was a second rainbow. It grew into the expansiveness, half of it crystalizing directly under and nearly touching the first one. Within minutes, the first rainbow began to fade, gently and then swiftly. And just before it disappeared, the second one began to dissolve even more quickly, melting into the atmosphere. In less than a minute, the rainbows were gone, so were the clouds, and the full sun owned the sky once again.

"This place is an awakening," I sighed, stepping a little higher on the ground toward the valley.

Fortunate timing allowed us to experience heaven's fractured light. The notion of emergence, of arrival, was primordial and ancient.

"Doesn't it seem like God is in this land?" I asked no one and everyone, my gaze remaining on the landscape. "Holiness is in wide open spaces."

We walked the road a bit, boots scraping the dusty earth. We inhaled and listened, and we traveled east through the valley. After a few miles, the road began to climb back up to the mountains, and at one turn, where the land plateaued for a short distance, a group of Native Americans had arranged several wooden tables near the road. The early evening light settled over jewelry made from silver, opal, and turquoise—bracelets, pendants, rings, and clasps of alabaster and lapis. On one table was a necklace, carrying a small bear carved out of black stone.

"It's the symbol of strength," said the sturdy young man seated behind one of the tables, proud of the goods before him. We were the only customers there now, likely the last of his day, maybe the only ones over the last several hours.

"And the stone?" I asked.

"Acoma," he said.

Acoma black jet is a fossilized wood, not unlike coal. A common stone used by the Navajo.

"It fights the spirits of depression and fear. It's a protective force. It refreshes the body," he said. "Is it for you?"

I hadn't thought about that, being drawn to the black bear for no clear reason.

"Well." I paused. "I think I might want to give it to my mother."

"Is she sick?"

My mother had been moved to a nursing home in Pennsylvania after home care was no longer realistic. She had suffered a long history of lung and blood ailments, and now dementia was eating away at her mind.

I paid him $20. He wrapped the bear in a soft white cloth, delicately folding it around the necklace and placing it in a small cardboard box.

My mother never hung crosses or framed depictions of Jesus on the walls of her home and never wore religious jewelry. My father kept a pendant, a stainless steel St. Christopher medal around his neck. He never took it off. Mom, however, was not one to outwardly exhibit her beliefs. She prayed in church and around the Thanksgiving table, and I remember hearing her whisper to God while she sat alone beside my father's bed days before cancer took him. She had faith, that enigmatic state of acceptance, but she rarely displayed it.

"I wish her serenity," the young man said. "And I wish you good journeys."

I thanked him and placed the cardboard box deep in the inside pocket of my suitcase. We took our places inside the RV and climbed farther into the mountains.

When I was a kid, playing Cowboys and Indians in the yards of my neighborhood—pretending to fight the natives, a toy revolver and holster strapped to my waist and a straw cowboy hat on my head—it never occurred to me that the savages believed in something. We fired pretend rounds of bullets at make-believe Indians, chasing them down in the woods across the street from my parents' small Cape Cod on a hill. We had no idea why we had to kill them; it was simply our job. If you were a cowboy, you shot Indians. We never considered that their souls might go to heaven. Decades later and years before traveling to the Navajo Nation, I was hiking at Starved Rock, a large state park along the south bank of the Illinois River about 100 miles from Chicago. I stepped along the trail that led to the top of an isolated sandstone butte. Not far from this great rock is the site of a combative 18th century tribal council meeting. As the legend goes, a brave from the Illinois tribe stabbed Chief Pontiac of the Ottawa tribe during the council. The reason for the attack is unclear, but it sparked revenge, and soon the tribes were in a bloody battle. The Illinois took refuge on the butte, and Pontiac's followers surrounded them. After many weeks, the Illinois starved to death on the rock. Standing on that ancient precipice hundreds of years later—above the flowing river and the tall maples hugging the cliffs—I could think not of the beauty before me, but only of death. The same way I did when I was a young cowboy shooting up the barbarians. Now, leaving the Navajo Nation, life, not death, was all that seemed to matter.

As the RV pulled us back to a four-lane road that would lead to a campsite for the night, we stayed quiet, a mixture of weariness and awe. Brad was behind the wheel, and the boys had settled on a bench in the RV's cabin. I stared out the passenger side window, occasionally glancing into the oversized side view mirror. It would be easy to dismiss and simple to label the late afternoon and evening as just one of the many special moments of a two-and-a-half week cross-country road trip through the

Rocky Mountains, the Salt Flats, Lake Tahoe, San Francisco, and Big Sur. But I knew better. Somewhere out there in the broad prehistoric land of America's southwest, where the foreground and background are impossible to distinguish, where long shadows cast by the sun appear to be tattooed on the far-reaching acres, where the moonlight tints red earth to a deep maroon, there are spirits—angels, Mother Nature's soldiers, Navajo gods. Whatever they are does not matter; what they're doing does. They dance in the corners of a another dimension, unseen but awaiting discovery, anticipating the right time and place to appear to those who are searching, to lay a hand on a shoulder of those who do not understand. Not to offer some inevitable truth or instill a faith that one does not deserve. It's not religious; it's not necessarily spiritual. It's, instead, deeply ancestral. It's the essence of a passage to peace, a home. It is the individual quest for a quiet place to watch the stars.

We arrived late at a dark and nearly silent campsite, the boys slept, one on the cabin bench, the other had moved to the bed in the rear of the RV. After backing our traveling home into a reserved space, Brad reached into the small cabinet behind the driver's seat and pulled out an unopened bottle of wine.

"A toast?" he asked.

I worked the corkscrew and poured the red blend into two clear plastic cups.

"Ever think about where you're supposed to be in the world?" I asked.

We tapped our cups and took our sips.

"All the time," he said.

"Did you go to church when you were a kid?" I asked.

"Oh yeah. Can't tell you the last time."

"Why does that happen?" I asked. "I look at people who are locked into their religion, their church. They seem pretty happy, don't they?"

"You're not thinking about going back to church, are you?" he smirked.

We drank two more classes of wine and corked what remained for another day. The next morning we would head for Albuquerque and Santa Fe through a long stretch of infinite land and a rumbling and flashing thunderstorm that forced us to pull off I-40 somewhere near Gallup and the Cibola National Forest. We sat in the RV on the scruffy desert land, the vehicle rocking in the high wind, and watched the horizontal lightning snap from cloud to cloud. Between thunder cracks, we heard the sound of a whistle, faintly masked by the weather. To the north of us, in the distance, was a freight train, traveling east. It chugged on toward an unknown destination and undoubtedly on a deadline. It had a schedule to meet, a place to be. Its route was clear. It did not matter that it may be heading away from or to its home; it had its definitive path of travel, presenting its own serenity. The whistle may have evoked a familiar melancholy born out of the belief that there is sadness in loneliness, but this did not matter. The crew knew where to take this train; the long ago laid track made certain of it. The train was solitary in the vast open land, in unforgiving weather, moving toward an end its crew would never question. The storm would eventually pass, the sky would clear, and the train would keep on running in the remoteness for a hundred more miles, distant but parallel to the highway, occasionally blowing its whistle, reminding us it was right alongside for as long as the track would allow.

Slow Ride

The King Street train station in Seattle is not in the best part of town. It's near the International District, a section of the city that has been in decline for years—gritty and neglected.

"Be careful down there," the driver said as I stepped from the bus at 3rd and Main in the middle of the afternoon.

Homeless men wrapped in blankets slept on the sidewalk. Groups of young and old men huddled together in the light rain, drinking from tall cans of beer in front of a convenience store and cigarette shop.

I was an hour early for my scheduled train, so I waited at a tavern a block from the station, nursing a pint of ale at the bar and eating clam chowder. The same college basketball game played on nearly all the dozen or so TVs.

"You from Chicago?" the bartender asked, eyeing the credit card I had given her. An image of the city's skyline on the plastic gave me away.

"I grew up in Aurora," she said. Aurora is a far west suburb of the city.

"My kids were raised in Naperville," I said.

"I went to Naperville North High School."

"The boys went to Central," I said.

"I love Seattle. But I'm still a Bears fan," she said, showing me the big Chicago C on her keychain.

"Heading back there," I said, standing to gather my backpack and jacket. "The slow way this time—by train."

"Always thought about that," she said. "I love road trips and that might be the ultimate."

I told her that I had driven from Chicago to Florida not too long ago to work at Jack Kerouac's House as the Writer-in-Residence for a summer and how it reminded me of all those road trips I took as a young man in a beat-up Chevy—Pennsylvania to Florida, Pittsburgh to Boston, up and down the Appalachian Mountains.

"I envy you," she said. "Too cool."

When I took the trip to Florida as an undergrad, it was nothing more than an adventure between semesters. In retrospect, it was much more. It was my first long journey as a young man, my first venture into freedom. Decades later, a 5000-mile cross-country road trip with my sons was sparked by middle-life unsettledness. That time, the freedom of the travel was needed to rebalance. Both trips delivered what was needed at the time.

Train travel was sparked by yet another reason. I had been working on a novel that involved a trip on the rails, so it would be research. I had never traveled this far on a train—three days, 2000 miles across the top of America. The only way I was going to understand this kind of journey was to actually do it and be with the people who traveled this way, those who lived far from airports and cities and sometimes far from anything.

It was almost 5 o'clock when I boarded The Empire Builder heading east. Going coach was the cheaper way, but maybe an upgrade to a sleeper car would have been a better idea, although a friend told me it wasn't worth it.

"Enjoy your excursion," the bartender said. A half-hour later, I had finished my beer and chowder and was off.

The train departed in the early evening, and the ride was quiet, even serene, and comfortable, the coach seats big and roomy but not necessarily made for sleep. I awakened several times overnight—1:33 a.m., 2:46 a.m., 3:36 a.m., 4:48 a.m., 6:10 a.m. At 6:30 a.m., I washed up in the restroom and brushed my teeth. The bathrooms were clean but tiny, bigger than an airplane's but just as cold and hard—made of chrome and steel, an uninviting industrial toilet was the centerpiece.

I was one of the first to enter the dining car. White linen covered the tables, fake flowers rested in clear vases in the center, and stainless steel utensils were tightly wrapped in cloth napkins. I was seated next to others. It is apparently a train custom to bunch travelers together either for convenience or to encourage community on moving steel.

Sylvester wore Levi's and a light denim shirt. He was a retired railroad worker. He told me he started as a laborer and went into management. "I take trains all the time," he said. "It's free, and I feel good here, moving like this, chugging along in some kind of rhythm."

We shared a morning of coffee and eggs with a young couple from Seattle, heading for White Fish, Montana to visit family. The couple was smart, friendly. She wore a Google t-shirt with an image of the Space Needle on the background. He wore a Pints of Pasta t-shirt. It had something to do with Portland. I didn't ask.

"I'm a Native American," Sylvester said. "I know Montana. It's beautiful in White Fish. Skiers love the area. I've worked this part of the country, repaired rail here. I know every inch of this track."

"What are the people like in Montana?" I asked.

"Good people. Ranchers. Smart," Sylvester said. "I grew up on a reservation."

"My brother lives in Montana," the man from the couple said. "There's a difference in West and East Montana."

"Wide open spaces in the East. Big country," said Sylvester, "but it's changing."

"More people?" I asked.

"Yes, but something is off, you know?" he said. "Last night a train hit a large herd of elk grazing on the tracks. Twenty-three dead animals. Too many elk. And too many people pushing them into places they shouldn't be."

I shook my head.

"Do you know what happens when a train going 60 miles-per-hour hits a big animal?" he asked. "They pretty much explode."

The woman from the couple grimaced.

"Can't even save the remains for meat," Sylvester added.

The train speakers interrupted. "Last call for White Fish," the voice said.

The couple rushed to grab their luggage and hurried to the train doors, leaving sausage links and half-eaten rye toast on their plates. White Fish had come up quickly. Sylvester said the train was ahead of schedule.

"Thank you for your time and the conversation," he said, standing and offering a handshake. "I wish you good travels."

For the next two hours, I sat in the observation car, writing in my journal, watching Montana go by—arrow straight pines stretching tall into the snowy sky against a backdrop of steep mountains. And for miles and miles, the scene through the large window hardly changed. There was no cell service. No homes tucked in the hills. An occasional road could be seen but no vehicles. Who wouldn't want to escape here? Who wouldn't want to find an individualized life in this wilderness? Even those marginalized men smoking and drinking in the shadows of Seattle's train station.

I rested my back against the seat, placed my boots on the metal rail just below the window, and waited patiently for what might come.

North Dakota needed a vacation from itself.

It was tired and worn, cold, bitterly cold. At 4 a.m. the temperature was -7 degrees. As the train pulled up to the station, the lights of the city were muted by crystalized snow, the kind that sparkles. No one was out, the station and the streets as barren as the landscape.

Freight trains had needed to pass somewhere in Eastern Montana, and our train had to pull off on a siding to permit them through. We had waited about forty-five minutes and we were now behind schedule. No one complained. If this had been an airline flight delayed on the runway at O'Hare, there would have been endless grumbling.

Last night before trying to sleep, I sat in the lounge car with the sofa seats and the big windows. I read in a book of travel essays about a journalist's trek to find an African tribe priest who had claimed he had cured AIDS. Across from me sat a young woman, maybe in her mid 20s—black hair, pale skin, a nose ring, and a tattoo on her neck. I could see the spine of the book she was reading—Tolstoy's *Anna Karenina*. Has she figured out the theme of trains in the novel? Does she know what Anna does to herself on the tracks of a train?

Train coffee is not as bad as you might think—better than what one gets in many of those Greek-run breakfast restaurants you find scattered around Chicago. It's not Metropolis or Intelligentsia, two of the city's beloved roasters. Still, it satisfies somehow. Maybe because it's all you have. There was no choice of coffee, and that lack of choice made me wonder about the passengers on the train—like the young man with the skull cap and the backpack who spoke to his daughter on his cell phone: *I'm on my way, little girl. It's just taking a little longer than Daddy hoped. I'll be there. Promise.* Or the man with mud on his jeans, wearing an old green flannel shirt and black cap, nursing a dark bruise under his eye, turning blue as it healed. Had he chosen his place in life? Or the silver-haired elderly woman dressed in her best skirt and blouse, and her shiniest earrings, sitting at a small table in the lounge, playing solitaire. Does she have options? And the girl with the tattoo and Tolstoy—did she have another book to read?

The train pulled away from Fargo. There was nothing to see out the windows, only darkness. Inside, people slept, snored, and wrapped themselves in blankets in coach chairs. Small green lights on the floor marked the way down the aisle to the bathroom, the lounge car, and dining car. From the front end of the train came the faint smell of coffee brewing, the earthy aroma of morning. When the diner hours began, I walked past sleepy travelers to ask for a cup. I chose cream, no sugar. And I sipped and savored, hoping the coffee would warm me as I waited for the sun to rise.

He looked like a heavy-set Floyd, the barber on "The Andy Griffith Show." He wore the same style of horn-rimmed glasses with the thin, silver metal at the bottom of the frames, same haircut, same slur to his words. He said, "right" a lot—a verbal tick.

"We're a few minutes outside St. Cloud," I said, an answer to his question about where we are on the line.

"Right," he said. "I can't see much in the dark of the morning here. And I just got up. But I know this line."

He liked talking about the Empire Builder and the towns it runs through.

"We're heading for St. Paul," he said, cutting into his pork sausage and sipping apple juice. He was directly across from me in the dining car. I looked at my phone. 6:35 a.m.

"That's where you're going? St. Paul?"

"Right," he said.

"Where you coming from?"

"Cut Bank."

"Montana?"

"Right."

"What's in Cut Bank?"

"Just wanted to see what I can see," he said. He smiled after nearly everything he said—a shy, quick grin. "I live in St. Paul." Another smile. "But I like the train."

I thought of Sylvester, the Native American, the old railroad worker.

"Cold up here," I said.

"Yes," he said. "How cold is it right now?"

I looked at my phone. "15 degrees," I said.

"That's not too bad," he said. "Born in Minnesota. I know cold." He laughed, pushed his sliding eyeglasses back up his nose. "There's no bad cold. It's just what it is."

"Well, it›s cold to me."

"Right." He looked out the window and sighed. "The stop before St. Cloud was Staples, North Dakota."

At Staples, an Amish family stood outside the station in the soft light of street lamps, waiting for the train doors to open. Several men in black brimmed hats gathered their luggage, and two women in bonnets nestled infants tight to their breasts. They moved slowly, as if the frigid weather would allow only deliberate motion, as if they would crack if they moved too quickly. They chose several seats behind me in coach, their luggage in the racks above. They spoke softly in what sounded like German. The babies cooed. Someone sang a lullaby.

"The Staples station is on the north side of the tracks," Floyd the barber said with a grin. "The St. Cloud station is on the south side of the tracks. And they go on like that. Back and forth."

"You *do* know this line," I said.

"Right."

It was the third day on the train. My last. I would be in Chicago in the late afternoon. But if I were a true train passenger—like Floyd—I would not be counting days or noting arrival times. I would, instead, be noticing on what side of the tracks the stations stood, how I slept, on what page I would return to my reading, and if my body was ready to eat the pork sausage they offered for breakfast in the dining car. This was not the kind of ride one takes in a hurry. Despite a schedule, despite the notation of exact departure and arrival times on every ticket, those on the train, although keenly aware of the element time plays on a journey such as this, are less concerned about its passage. Time is not something to maintain or adhere to here, not for the passenger. It is instead, only a marker, the clock's stamp on individual moments.

In St. Paul, the train's power went out. We switched locomotives, and the crew had to unplug the train's electrical generators for a few minutes. The coach car fell oddly quiet—engine off, heat off, the hum of movement on the rails was no longer. I could hear only soft breathing, the creak of vinyl seats as people adjusted their bodies in them, the crinkle of plastic being removed from a packaged breakfast muffin, and the sigh that comes after a sip of coffee in a paper cup—sounds that had been muted in the chug of rail travel. A few passengers stepped out for a smoke on the platform, others to stretch. This was also where Floyd departed. He passed my seat in coach.

"You enjoy your day, now," he said, smiling. "The next stop after Minneapolis is Red Wing."

I checked the schedule. Floyd was right.

The power returned in a few minutes, and the conductor announced the "all aboard." We were again in motion.

At La Crosse, we crossed the Mississippi, more frozen and wider than anyone who has never seen it could imagine. And at the La Crosse station, the Amish stepped out of the train, and the party stepped on—about a dozen people, each holding a beer bottle. The mix of men and women were in their early 30s, one of them blasted Neil Diamond from a portable speaker, presumably connected to a smartphone.

"Sweet Caroline! Good times never seemed so good!!!"

They took their position in the back of the lounge car and ordered a bottle of wine and more beer. The conductor, a burly man dressed in his navy blue uniform and cap, greeted them warmly, took their tickets, and asked where they were headed.

"Chicago!" they screamed and raised their drinks. "To debauchery!" someone belted. More cheers.

One man in the group asked to take a selfie with the conductor. He agreed. The partier asked if one of the women could sit on his lap. "This is not going viral, is it?" he asked.

They cheered again. "To the conductor!" A woman with blonde hair and what appeared to be Mardi Gras beads around her neck took her seat on the conductor's knee and wrapped her arms around his bearded neck. Another cheer, many smiles, and the clicks of smartphone cameras.

We were 300 miles from Chicago.

I found a quieter spot. I read a new book on my iPad—*A Paris Apartment* by Michelle Gable, a novel about the treasures discovered inside an abandoned apartment in the French city. Across the aisle from me, a husband and wife argued about meeting friends for dinner. She wanted to; he didn't. "Who will feed your horses if we go out?" he asked. There were a number of couples—what appeared to be husbands and wives—on this stretch of the trip, some young and some old. Some sat together, up close in the lounge seats, holding hands. Others were separated by the tabletops of their booths, saying little to each other. This couple sat together on one side of a booth. "The horses will be okay," she answered. She touched his hand and smiled.

The cackles from the rowdy crowd in the back cascaded to the front of the lounge car. The partiers sang Pink Floyd's "Wish You Were Here." The volume grew as others in the group joined in. A man in a blue denim shirt and CAT hat walked by the drinkers and towards me.

"If that's the tavern back there," he said, pointing to the crowd, "then this must be the library."

I nodded.

I was ready for Chicago. Not tired of the travel, the humming motion, the noisy party, or the marginal food; I just needed to step out and walk. Really walk. There's a lot of sitting on a train. Three days with little movement can exhaust you. Still, inside the big steel horse, I had found comfort wrapped in a thick blanket made from the swaths of America. I was motionless, yet full of motion. I was alone, but not. I was content, yet entombed in a mist of solitude, the kind you find in church that is at the same time peaceful and disquieting.

The wide-open spaces of the West and all of what that offers the spirit slipped away as I headed east. There's a book

I truly love. And I offer it to anyone who sees the connection between the human condition and the harshness of dense populations—Gretel Ehrlich's *The Solace of Open Spaces*. I thought of it somewhere between Columbus and Milwaukee and I wondered if each of us is often like a train and the ride it offers: quiet and brooding, accommodating and mighty, scheduled and tardy, journeying, chugging, and intermittently at rest.

The conductor called for Chicago.

"This is the last stop on the Empire Builder!" He suggested we check our baggage and connections at Union Station and said something about Red Cap service, whatever that was.

The last of the passengers were all around me—a mix of couples, traveling businessmen, students, revelers, and Amish families heading for a connection to Pennsylvania. The crew gathered trash and collected the white cloth covers that protected the seats' headrests. The lounge area was closed. The drinkers and the singers were silent and in their seats in another one of the cars. Some slept. In the distance was a big, hard, sulking city, and in the rear view mirror was what Kerouac had written about—*all that raw land*. And in the vastness of it all, I couldn't help think about what Jack considered, how none of us ever knows what will happen to us tomorrow, tonight, or an hour from now. We plan, we schedule, we prepare, we organize, we arrange, but we can only be sure of the present moment, the here and now. For three days, the train car was that *present moment*, my cabin and my cradle, and I believed in it.

The train rocked like a lullaby as it entered Union Station. The pungent smell of grease and diesel, the familiar screech of steel wheels on steel track, and the rush of that unmistakable Chicago air, chilly and damp, embraced me. As I stepped from the train, I thought about the waitress in the bar in Seattle with the big C on her keychain who had told me how she envied my trip, how she missed Chicago, her hometown, but had found a kind of sanctuary in the Northwest. And I considered all I would now forever carry with me—the tangible spirits of those I had witnessed and met, the brief but nevertheless lasting encounters, fading yet lingering along the tracks, stretching out over my shoulder and disappearing now in the day's last light.

Iowa

I was to meet her in person at a corner bakery. She arrived before me, waited at the table by the window, and smiled as I came through the revolving glass door.

"Leslie?" I asked.

"Yes," she said, standing to shake my hand, still smiling.

"Do you mind if I grab a coffee?"

"Absolutely. Go right ahead."

Leslie told me months afterward that she watched me move to the counter that morning, watched me fill my mug and pay, observing what she believed was a manner of quiet confidence. She said she could tell immediately that I was exactly who I said I was.

We met on Match, the online dating portal. It was an awkward introduction. I had reached out first but had posted only the most minimal information about me on the site. More importantly, I had not included a photo. As a college teacher and a journalist, people might know my name; there might be students online. This seemed a justifiable reason for no photo, but not posting a picture signaled an alarm for many. *He's a creeper, a cheater, a less-than-truthful person.* That's what a photo-less profile carried with it—stigma. But my first online message to her was sincere, she said, and she took the chance, reading all she could about me on my personal website and online, where she found plenty of pictures. She even read one of my books before we met. "I think every Match date should write a memoir," she later said.

My life was an open book.

What about Leslie? There was no book. No personal website. I read her Match profile several times over, and after a series of emails, we began talking on the phone every few days. I soon learned all I needed to do was to ask the right questions to open up her world. There was no pretense. She was honest, real. There was a delicate smile in her voice.

"Full disclosure," she wrote in one of the first emails before talking on the phone. "I'm actually in Iowa."

Match links people in a geographical radius chosen by the user. I did not choose Iowa. But Leslie had listed towns in the Chicago area, where I lived, so our profiles came up. She had planned to move back to the area and was buying a house. She asked if we could meet in person when she was in town.

That's how it was decided, a morning meeting at the corner bakery on the day she would be heading back to Iowa City from Chicago. I was interested in Leslie. I wouldn't have talked with her so many times on the phone or agreed to get together. She also was interested in me, I thought. She had answered my phone calls, laughed at my attempts at wit. However, she did tell me later that she chose the bakery because it was close to the highway where she could make a perfect escape if things didn't go well, in case the guy with no photo really was a creeper.

Our phone talks had revealed an intelligent woman, one with a warm heart and a gentle emotional side, someone with deep colors in her soul, someone who felt things intensely. There was more to learn, of course, and there was a lot to get to know beyond the niceties and good behavior of those early conversations. And there was the question of Iowa. Under all the usual uncertainties of a new relationship, I wondered. *Why had she been in Iowa?* Why did she move from where she grew up, her lifelong home, where she raised her children, where her aging parents lived, where she played tennis in the afternoon sun, where she put her hands in the dirt to plant spring flowers? What did she leave? From what did she run? For me, Iowa was nothing more than the state west of Illinois—cornfields, pig farms, *Field of Dreams*, Madison County's covered bridges. I once drove through Iowa on my way to California. There were more rolling hills than I had anticipated, but for the most part, the state was forgettable. There was little of weight in Iowa, nothing significant in its history to hold it in place, nothing to lure you. Even the pioneers steered their wagons straight through when trudging west. California had the Gold Rush. Iowa? How could it compare?

"Iowa was my sabbatical," Leslie confessed during one of our phone conversations. "I needed peace. I found it there."

Leslie's face was framed by the morning light filtering through the bakery's window, backlighting her as if she were on stage before an audience of one. She wore a mushroom colored sweater with a paisley scarf around her neck; her dark blonde hair was highlighted and fell to her tightly angled shoulders. She had big eyes, narrow fingers. There was a simple ring on her right hand.

I placed my coffee mug on the table across from her tea and sat down.

"So, you're not in class today?" Leslie asked.

"I'll go in later. Afternoon session," I said. "No rush. Sorry I was a little late."

Leslie told me she was drawn to teachers. Her daughter taught grade school in Iowa.

"Tell me what you teach?" she asked.

"Writing classes. I teach journalism and broadcast work."

"Oh yes," she said, remembering an exchange on the phone. "I remember the writing, obviously. Freshman?"

"Mostly upper level. A lot of seniors." I tried to sound modest but impressive.

She was even prettier than her photos, and it unsettled me.

"And you are back in town to finish the house deal?" I asked.

Leslie had sold her home in Iowa City and was buying in the Chicago area. She had been a real estate agent for years and was working through the process with the confidence of someone who had done this for others many times over.

"Yes. But I have to get back to Iowa," she said. "Not that I'm trying to hurry things, though," she laughed.

"Well, I hope not," I said.

Our spot in the bakery was now our own singular world—no silverware clinking, no dishes clanking, no whir of an espresso machine, no customer conversation. We continued to talk. Children. Parents. Where we grew up. We built on some of our earlier phone conversations. Leslie—tennis. David—golf. Baseball. Gardening. Football. Red wine. Kerouac. Europe. Thoreau. The scene we both loved in the movie *Almost Famous*—on the bus, everyone singing "Tiny Dancer."

"What kind of music do you listen to?" I asked.

"Indie. Folk. Americana."

"I'm all over the place. I love Dylan."

"Have you ever heard of Dawes?"

"I love Dawes. I just saw them last fall at the Chicago Theatre."

Leslie leaned backward and then toward me. There was a little gasp.

"Oh my," she said. "You know Dawes? No one our age knows Dawes. I love them."

A fragment of her heart was revealed. Chest bones opened. We had discovered mutual touchstones elsewhere, but music—it exposed her. In an instant, we were recalling the lyrics that made us cry, and the songs that made us tremble.

She titled her head and adjusted her scarf, the window light reflected off the ring on her finger. "We must be the only people over fifty who know Dawes. Amazing."

"It won't be long," I said. "They're too good."

We kept talking. Yoga. High schools. First Communions. Hiking. Colorado. Pittsburgh. Photography. Picasso. Bikes. Health.

"You know, I've been through a bit," Leslie said. She slipped her hand under her scarf, shifting the fabric to one side. "Thyroid cancer." On her neck was a blotch of red mixed with damaged flesh. The skin appeared singed. "Stage four. Radiation."

I paused. Swallowed.

"I was supposed to die. But I didn't," she said.

Leslie measured my response. It was not what she had said that made me uneasy, it was how she looked as she told me. She had broken a seal, pushed away a curtain. She was naked now. I thought about my grandparents, my mother and father, my sister and how their deaths changed my sense of belonging to something, to someone. Now there was Leslie, who had stood at the edge of her mortality, and I was frightened. I might lose her, I thought. A woman I hardly knew.

"I'm going to live." Her voice was nearer now; I could feel her breath.

Iowa. This is why. It was her place to heal.

The bakery reawakened. Two women behind me giggled over tea, a server called orders, a spoon fell from the coffee counter. Sounds encased me, layered by the life in the room. Our table by the window had rejoined the world.

"I'm very happy to hear that," I said, knowing my reply was hopelessly inadequate. *What does one say to another who has come so close to death? Tell your own story?*

"I had a health scare, too," I said.

Leslie's eyes widened.

How silly of me to bring up the heart attack? Predictable. Dumb. It was a reflex reaction. Whose health concerns were the most troubling?

"Very mild," I said. "They put in a stent."

It happened one morning while out working a story for a news radio station about a series of muggings in a Northwest Chicago neighborhood. There was deep chest congestion, heavy sweating. I drove myself to the hospital, was wheeled down the emergency room hallway. The surgery I could watch on a monitor. And as the stent was put in place, relief came immediately. The doctor told me I was lucky.

"Two weeks later I rode my bike twelve miles. Probably shouldn't have so soon. But I felt fine."

"Well, I am also very happy to hear that," Leslie said, repeating my words. "We've both overcome."

I put my hands together, interlocking my fingers, and leaned in. "Tell me more about Iowa."

It was on a Sunday morning not long after packing up her life in Chicago, shaking off the scars, and moving to Iowa City that Leslie noticed the scullers, quietly gliding on the Iowa River. The river ran just a short distance from her cottage home where she walked her dog most days. Leslie watched as the four-person crew propelled the boat through a series of drives and recoveries, a synchronized motion of oars in and out of the water. The rowers were young, maybe university students, maybe a team. *I'm in pretty good shape,* she thought. *Sure, I'm fifty years old but I do yoga. I want to do that.*

From a wooden launching dock, the instructor snapped out commands, encouragement over a bullhorn. And on the water, alone in a boat, Leslie held tight to the fiberglass oars. It was her first lesson.

"Catch and finish," barked the instructor, a young woman in her early twenties who had helped the university's team. "Feather the blades."

Sweat formed on Leslie's shoulders and forearms. Her concentration was on overdrive, never noticing the hawk overhead or the group of college students walking along the riverbank. To balance took all her focus. It was hard work even with pontoons attached to the starboard and port sides. *It still could tip over,* Leslie thought.

"Square your blades," shouted the instructor.

Leslie's orange life vest constrained her, mildly constricting the stroke. But it also calmed her, hugging her body like a caring friend. With every motion, Leslie attempted to replicate what she had been taught on the riverbank—the proper grip of the oars, the mechanics of the stroke, the use of the muscles in her arms and her legs. *Dig in, Leslie,* she commanded herself. *You can do this. You WILL do this.* Balance is what she sought, and she was going to find it. Balance was freedom, about choosing to be awake and alive enough for magic to happen. But to know this, Leslie had to launch into the steady current of the Iowa River and work heavy oars in and out of deep enough water that could—if she tumbled in—swallow her.

The next night, Leslie's friends—a professor of engineering and his wife—who lived next door in the Manville Heights neighborhood, invited Leslie to the outdoor concert in the ped mall in downtown Iowa City. They walked there after dinner, following a shortcut known by only a few. Old hippies, professors from the university, summer-soaked children, and college students crowded the outdoor space. They drank sodas and ate hotdogs and big salty pretzels. From the far end of the mall came the music—a lively electric bass wrapped in congas and psychedelic guitar. Bambu played funky Afro-Latin songs. The singer was from Kingston, Jamaica, the percussionist from Argentina, the guitarist had roots in New Jersey rock, and the keyboardist was a California boy. The music commanded your body to move, so Leslie's neighbor jumped into the space in front of the stage, swaying her arms and swinging her hips, her eyes closed, her head tilted back. She floated as if her feet were drifting just above the concrete plaza. Others joined—a little girl, maybe ten years old, tossed her hair and swirled her body in circles. An older couple—a woman with silver hair and beads around her neck, and a man in cargo shorts and a Pink Floyd t-shirt—held each other's hands as they twirled together in the late day sun.

"She does this all the time," said the husband, watching his wife melt into the moment.

Leslie eyes were on her friend. There was such freedom in her movement—so unselfish and honest, as if something mystical had taken over, something far bigger than her. The music shifted to a conga rhythm and a trippy, intoxicating guitar, and a few others joined the dreamy dancing. Leslie's friend smiled and beckoned with a wave.

In that instant, in the wake of that tiny gesture, Leslie was someone new, inviting herself to be vulnerable, to be exposed, to be true to the world, to liberate herself. The morning on the river had jump-started something deep; the fear of plunging under the water had stirred her. And so she stepped forward into the music and began to dance . . . with her friend, with herself, with the universe.

We sat in a dimly lit booth near the back of the restaurant, a white tablecloth draped under our dishes. Leslie sipped wine; I nursed a double espresso.

"I hope it's not a deal breaker," she said, "especially after I've brought you here to one of Iowa City's finest."

I shook my head. "Of course not. No one's path is perfect."

"It's part of the reason I'm here, of course," she said. "Iowa."

"I can see that," I said.

"At first, Iowa was my escape, but now I know it was not that at all. It was instead, my place to search, search for me."

She had walked away from two marriages, from two men who held conditions on love, men who never grew up, men who took advantage, men who raged.

"Who says we're always supposed to get it right," I said.

Two weeks before the dinner and a few weeks after meeting at the corner bakery, I had asked Leslie if she might consider me visiting her in Iowa before she left for good. I insisted I would stay in a hotel. If we were to be something together, I wanted to see and understand her world in Iowa. I wanted to know what it meant.

Later than night, after dinner, we would have a drink at Stella, a bar just up the street from the university's stadium, and under a street lamp in the parking lot, I would kiss Leslie for the first time. I would sleep that night in her lower-level guest bedroom and awake early and feed her cat fishy food from a can. And in the quiet early morning, I would sit on her living room couch by the window and I would read, and when she awoke, she would rush down the stairs from her second-floor bedroom, whisking by, never seeing me there. She would hurry to the kitchen to make certain I had not let her indoor cat out the backdoor, and when she finally noticed me, she would thank me for taking care of the aging pet. We would have omelets and pancakes and linger over coffee at the Hamburg Inn on Linn Street. She would drive me through campus, take me to the big house where her son lived with other students, and we'd ride past the campus buildings where her daughter had once attended classes just a few years earlier. We'd walk by the Iowa Writer's Workshop and step inside Prairie Lights Books, where some of my books would soon be placed on the store's shelves. She would show me the tree-lined golf course where she challenged herself with a new sport and hit balls for hours on a grassy practice range. And she'd walk me along the river where she had learned to row and show me the ped mall where she had learned to dance again.

"Why leave?" I asked, ordering another coffee as we talked after dinner.

"It's time," she said. "Iowa was my adopted home, no question, but the shiny penny, well, it has dulled a bit."

"Newness gone?"

"I want to leave while the beauty of what it was for me is still fresh, still shiny," she said. "It was a new place under a new sky. But the same stars are up there, you know, no matter where you are."

Living in Iowa was never about forever, not some deep rooted home of stone. And Leslie did not arrive without tears. Crying was necessary. She knew this. Iowa allowed her to leave things behind and discover a place to open up again. Moving there was not about achieving goals or a new place to tick off a do-over checklist. It was easy to explain her time in Iowa as a kind of spiritual getaway, a life reset, a work of restoration. But she knew differently. She knew it was more. Iowa was about becoming. It was about shedding skin, revival, selfish independence, gritty and wondrous newness, about space and time—space to let the heart stretch, time to become young again. And now the day had come for Leslie to pack it all up and carry Iowa with her while its flowers were still in bloom.

We returned to Leslie's house after dinner and the drink at Stella under the subdued glow of a half-moon. I don't recall the stars that evening, if it had been clear enough to see any, but through the front window came a glint of light from the table lamp Leslie had lit before leaving. It wasn't bright enough to illuminate the stones and a clear path from the driveway to her door, but it was enough to point the way—our North Star, our Polaris, holding steady while the rest of the world swirled around us.

Silverfish

My tenant sent me a text that included a phone photo of a grayish-blue insect. It looked like a tiny, slimy crawfish with long antennae and feelers along the sides of its body. The message underneath read: *They r everywhere!*

I replied with my own text: *Everywhere? Or just in sink and counter?*

Disgusting, he replied.

Silverfish. I knew it when I saw the photo. A few months before, there had been a small, undetected leak under the kitchen sink. It apparently had been dripping for quite a while. Silverfish love moisture. They avoid light. The dark, damp space below the sink was a good home.

I could see on the phone that my tenant was typing another message.

Wife is freaking out.

I'll call someone, I replied and immediately telephoned an exterminator. The silverfish would have to leave and find somewhere else to live or face death by chemical.

The silverfish and the text changed everything for me. In that moment, I knew I was done being a landlord; I knew it was time to get rid of the bugs and sell the place. What I was not expecting was how tough it would be to say goodbye.

When I lived in the thirty-year-old, three-bedroom house, I had my share of homeowner headaches. There was a leak in the drain of the upstairs tub. It had left water stains on the living room ceiling. The wood trim along the roof outside the house and around the chimney had rotted to the point of falling off and needed to be replaced and repainted. One of my trees, a big maple, had grown tall enough to snake a sizeable limb out over the wooden fence and just inches above my neighbor's backyard shed. "You gonna trim that tree soon?" he asked. I hired a rough-and-tumble guy who showed up in his beat-up Ford truck with a big ladder and a handsaw. He was maybe sixty years old and walked with a limp. "You have insurance, right?" I asked. "You bet," he said. I watched him work with a high level of anxiety. Then there was the robin that got in the house. In its panic, the bird shit all over two walls in the living room, the floor near the dining room fireplace, and around two large windows near the entrance. After trying for hours to coax the bird out the front door, it finally found its way through the sliding glass door to the patio. I used two bottles of Windex and a big container of disinfectant.

I bought the house after my divorce. My former wife found it. It was just two blocks from the house where we had all lived together. "The kids can walk here," she said, hoping I would go along with living so close. I did. Her plan was my plan. Our divorce carried its pain, but we were determined to be grownups and wanted to try to do the best for everyone, especially the boys.

The night I moved in to the place, the boys came over to sleep. All the furniture hadn't been delivered yet, so we stretched out sleeping bags on the living room floor. They brought their dog. I made popcorn and popped open cans of soda, and we watched movies on TV until we fell asleep. I had given the boys carte blanche to decorate their individual bedrooms at the house. "You can paint it anything you want," I said. Casey picked orange. I think the paint color was called tequila sunrise. We covered all four walls. "I want black," Graham said. "*Solid* black?" I asked. He reminded me about my offer to allow the boys to do what they wanted. We compromised. Two black walls and two deep red, blood red. Years later, the walls were repainted off-white. It took three coats to cover the orange and five coats to hide the red and black.

The boys continued to come over from time to time and sometimes stayed the night, but it was infrequent during high school and afterward. They had better things to do than to hang out at Dad's. Still, the house was a good place at the right time, and it served its purpose for me. My sister and I laid laminate flooring in the dining room and living room. I repainted the mantel around the fireplace, painted the garage floor, resurfaced the black asphalt driveway, and rearranged the furniture. I rearranged again when a girlfriend and her son moved in and changed it back to the original when they moved out. I watched two Super Bowls, three Masters, and dozens of Cubs games on a new big screen television, another promise to my sons. I tore out two overgrown evergreen bushes near the garage, planted marigolds along the walkway every season, and rooted a clematis vine near the front porch. In the spring it bloomed blue.

I lived alone in the house much of the time I was there, and when the boys began to go off to build their own lives, I had the urge to pull my world even closer. The house now seemed far too big, more than I wanted to deal with. I sold half of my furniture, dozens of books, donated old pots to Goodwill, gave away the lawnmower, and left behind all the garden tools, window treatments, and ceiling-high shelving in the garage. I kept my leather couch and chair, queen bed, clothes, the books I cherished, my guitar, and stacks of CDs. I found a renter and moved into a one-bedroom apartment two towns away. It was in one of those sprawling suburban complexes with a courtyard and a common area for game nights and bring-your-own bottle Friday evening happy hours. It was soulless, but it was simple, and I wanted simple.

My first tenant was a divorced man in his 40s. He carried with him far too much furniture and a lot of expensive artwork. He also brought along his big golden retriever, and when he left after two years, two years worth of dog shit remained in the backyard. I kept his deposit until he cleaned it up. A young family from the city rented next. They had been living in an apartment complex for several years. The two young children could walk to the elementary school and play in their own fenced-in yard.

During the first two years as a landlord, I considered selling the place, but the real estate market would not cooperate. I was under water and it would be a long recovery from the down period. Renting would at least pay the monthly mortgage. After nearly ten years, housing prices began to rise, and it was time. Yes, the silverfish text sealed the plan to sell the place, but there had been plenty of landlord emergencies—the late night phone call in the bitter month of February when the thermostat would only reach 55 degrees, the time the water heater burst and spilled gallons into the kitchen, the scorching July afternoon when the air conditioning unit died, the week a persistent washing machine leak poured water through a laundry room wall and into the kitchen pantry, destroying my tenant's stored pasta and Cheerios, the late summer violent hailstorm that forced a new roof and new gutters. I was weary.

Leslie helped me get the house ready for sale. She knew how to price it, stage it, market it, and with all her years in real estate, I knew I was in good hands. She held mine when I needed it, calmed me when I was frustrated, straighten my thinking when I was off base about how to negotiate the offers. The process was quite smooth, and you would think I would be thrilled that it took only three days to sell the place, that I had a buyer who was beside himself to win a minor bidding war, and that a large part of the profit from the sale of the house would now help me pay off my son's nagging student debt. But passing off the keys for good would force a door to close, shut it tight, and lock it. That place—my one-time home—those times, inside and out—all those moments were going away.

When I graduated from college, I came back to my childhood home to live for a few months and later found an apartment about twenty minutes away. I had been living nearly a hundred miles away from home for four years, and returning to my small bedroom on the second floor of the old house could only be temporary, although there was no doubt I loved the French toast my mother made in the mornings and the ready-to-wear ironed shirts in the closet, and I appreciated how my father washed my car for me twice a week, his soapy hands in a bucket and smile on his face. But I was nearly 23 years old and had a job working at a local country radio station. It was time to have my own space.

I don't remember much about that first apartment. You think I would. I recall the cute girl who lived across the hall, but that's about it. After a couple of years, I purchased my first house, a new townhome six miles farther from the city. The contractor was a shyster and tried to skimp on some of the agreed-upon trim and ceramic tile work. He also tried to get away with a poorly poured concrete driveway. When my father saw it, he insisted I refuse to close on the place until they repaired it. I did and the contractor did. I was there for a couple of years before moving to Chicago and living in a friend's studio apartment on the city's north side and then a condo west of the city before my then-wife and I built a colonial in the suburbs and started a family.

We may move in to these places, these temporary homes of ours, for the neighborhood, for the schools, the number of bedrooms, the fenced-in backyard, the two-car garage, the garden, the nearby bus stop, the inexpensive rent, but we stay because we have fallen in love. And when it is time to leave, we leave behind parts of ourselves, losing them to time. Still, energy remains, the spirit stays, and those who next inhabit that space, if they allow their hearts to be open, will be nourished.

The life of a landlord and the texts of creepy insects are behind me now. But I wonder if the new owner of my old home might ever strip away the paint in the bedrooms and wonder why someone would coat the walls with the colors of tangerine orange, deep red, and the black of the deepest reaches of outer space.

Cuba

The road to the beach was closed. A white police vehicle was parked on the shoulder, another partially blocked the street, and a trio of Cuban authorities, members of the Policía Nacional Revolucionaria—the National Revolutionary Police Force—in gray and black uniforms, stood nearby, one in the middle of the road. He watched us move closer, pointed an index finger at the car, and motioned sharply to his left. We were being ordered to pull over.

"Hmm," said Renaldo, our driver. "Something's up."

My two sons and I had just arrived in the Cuban city of Trinidad after several days in and around Havana and were hoping to swim in the clear sea along the beach at Ancón, one of Cuba's more beautiful stretches of coastline. In the previous days, we had immersed ourselves in cigars and rum, silky black beans and sweet plantains, the sights of strikingly beautiful women, giant ceiba trees, royal palms, and the taste of sugar cane. We walked in Hemingway's footsteps and drank the liquor he drank. We had swayed to Cuban rhythms at every turn and had come to Trinidad to see the centuries old colonial city, climb its towers, and stay with a Cuban family in a small cement home painted Caribbean green on a cobblestone street near the Plaza Mayor. Renaldo was our guide, a pleasant man in his 40s, fast to notice what he referred to as a "cañón"—a young Cuban woman with plenty of curves, explosive, and "fumar calliente." He was also quick to smile, but that smile now seemed like a mask as he moved the car in the direction of the policeman's finger.

"Is everything okay?" Casey asked, turning toward Renaldo. My oldest son, the tallest of us, had taken the front passenger seat for the long, bumpy drive from Havana to gain as much comfort as possible.

Renaldo hesitated, his eyes remaining on the road and the officer. "I don't know," he said.

While planning this trip, my sons and I had joked about being arrested by the Cuban "Federales," which is not the word for the Cuban authorities or even correct Spanish. "Federales" was popularized in movies like *The Wild Bunch* and *The Treasure of Sierra Madre*. In the Spanish language the word is "federal" with the stress on the last syllable and Mexican authorities are called Policía Federal, not the "Federales." Each of us had traveled to many places before, separately and together, but Cuba was still in many ways a forbidden land to Americans.

The officer approached the driver-side window, and Renaldo rolled it down. The heat rolled through the opening like an ocean wave.

For what seemed like several minutes, Renaldo and the officer spoke in Spanish. Casey, Graham—my younger son—and I remained quiet, eyes on their mouths as if we might somehow be able to translate. We knew little Spanish, although Casey was recalling some of what he had learned in high school years ago. Still, not enough to discern what was occurring before us.

I had been long for Cuba. Since my university days studying Hemingway's writing, fishing, and his tumultuous love life on the island, I had been in her charms. Cuba—its violent and passionate politics, its revolutions, its dictators and freedom fighters, the lure of its vices—had me good. My man-crush on Ernesto "Che" Guevara was not love at first sight. It came to be cemented only after reading *The Motorcycle Diaries,* the story of his revolutionary coming of age, traveling in South America in 1952 as a 23-year old medical student from Buenos Aires on a gasping and stammering 1939 Norton 500cc. He and his friend, Alberto Granado, planned to see the land and the people they had read about in college history books. Instead, they unexpectedly discovered the oppressed, the marginalized, and the sick. It changed Ernesto. It changed everything. He joined Fidel Castro to liberate Cuba from a military dictatorship. Like so many others, Che's idealism made an impression on me, although the realities of his revolution never matched the dreams. Still, with all of this, I knew I wanted to visit Cuba before it changed. Fidel was dead. Raul, his brother, was now in power and appeared more open to the world. The U.S. was slowly loosening fifty-year-old trade embargoes. Time was of the essence. Get to Cuba while it was still magically trapped in a bottle, before Starbucks took over every corner in Havana.

"Gracias," said Renaldo, rolling up the car window. "Chao."

We sat in anticipation as Renaldo turned the car toward the short road to the right.

"So?" I asked from the rear seat.

"Drugs," Renaldo said. "They found cocaine. Packages all over the beach."

Graham sighed. He had wanted most of all to swim in the warm waters.

"They are checking everything, everyone," Renaldo said. "But, no worry. This is a beach here." He pointed out the windshield. Some three hundred meters down the road was another beach—rockier, less sandy than Ancón. "It's for the locals," he said.

"I'm okay with that," I said. "I kind of prefer it. Don't you guys?"

"Let's do it," Graham said. Casey nodded.

"And we're all okay, right?" I asked.

Renaldo gave the thumbs up.

The beach was narrow and covered in small stones that looked like gray coral and crushed shells. Casey took photos with an antique Leica camera he'd purchased for the trip and found a spot to sun himself. Graham and I navigated ten meters of rocky ocean bottom before reaching soft sand, and for about an hour, we jumped over and over to avoid the rough waves. The water was clear and warm. The air smelled of salt. From a small cabana came salsa music. Three men and four women danced barefoot in the sand, rum swirling in the clear plastic glasses that they held in their hands.

Graham and I had forgotten towels, so we let the sun dry us as best it could and knocked sand from our feet before stepping into the car.

"Good swim?" Renaldo asked. He had been waiting near the car, probably admiring the "cañón."

"Great," I said.

"Perfect," said Graham.

Renaldo was again at the wheel and tried to exit the small parking area by a different road than before, but a rusted metal gate blocked us. He turned down the short road where we had earlier entered and again found the police. An officer, his uniform shirt unbuttoned several holes from the neck, motioned for Renaldo to stop.

"Una vex más," Renaldo said.

"One more time," Casey translated.

This was a different officer than before, and this time Renaldo greeted him with a handshake through the open window. *Did he know him? Was it a sign of respect?* I couldn't imagine reaching out my hand to shake that of a state trooper during a highway stop on any road in America.

Again, there was a lot of Spanish, but this time the exchange was short and matter-of-fact.

"He wants to search the car," Renaldo said. "Stay here." He stepped out and shut the door.

"Great," Graham said.

"This is interesting," Casey added.

I had been calm through the earlier encounter, but now it all seemed more serious, foreboding.

"We don't have anything back there, do we?" I asked, thinking of the trunk, of any rum we may have purchased that was somehow, some way illegal. "Nothing, right?" I asked again, thinking this time of weed. Graham and Casey had smoked before in the U.S., so had I, but they had assured me they wouldn't be so stupid as to try to bring any to Cuba on a cultural visa or so crazy as to try to buy some on the island.

"Jesus," Graham grumbled. "No."

"Dad, really," Casey added.

"Sorry. Parent mode."

None of us turned around to watch what was going on at the rear of the car. Instead, I kept my eyes forward, glancing at the rearview mirror. I could see the open trunk lid and shadows moving across the gap of light where the hinges met the car's body.

With the swift sound of metal latching on metal, the car rocked slightly as the policeman shut the trunk. Through the mirror, I could see Renaldo smiling at the officer. I heard muffled Spanish, and in a moment, Renaldo was at the driver-side door.

"Gracias," Renaldo said as the officer moved toward his previous post and waved us on. Renaldo slipped into his seat and reached for the seatbelt. As we pulled out to the road that would return us to Trinidad, he nodded to the officer, and just as the car sped up, Renaldo pointed his thumb at Casey.

"He's guilty!" Renaldo laughed. "That's what I would have told him."

"That's not funny," Casey snapped.

"Then it was them!" Renaldo said, pointing to Graham and me.

I immediately thought of the new U.S. embassy in Havana. The city tour guide had pointed it out to us two days earlier.

The road to the beach at Ancón was restricted for the rest of the daylight hours and presumably into the evening, maybe even the next day. Police were said to have been all over the beach and in and out of the nearby resort for many hours. But the heart of Trinidad, a few kilometers away, was quiet and peaceful, and that night, on a patio under the sprawling branches of an ancient ceiba tree—the Afro-Cuban symbol of maternal healing—we ate our dinners of peppers and rice, black beans, pork, chicken, flan, and Cuban chocolate ice cream. The menu noted we could pay with American dollars, an unusual opportunity, but the proprietor insisted on a converted price that was exorbitant. We chose instead our remaining CUC—Cuban Convertible Peso. It seemed only right in the end. And before leaving for a night at our host family's home, I signed the restaurant's patron book, noted that we were Americans, and gave thanks for the food, the day's bright sun, the warm sea, and the goodness of people. After all, we were in Trinidad, the city of the holy trinity.

Early the next morning, I met Casey on the patio of our host family's house. He sat in a cane rocker, reading a book about

American Indians. Near him was a rectangular table already dressed with three place settings. Tatiana and her mother worked in the tiny kitchen just off the small living space in the front of the house. Each day the summer air had been an espresso made with raw sugar, thick and heavy but still sweet and recuperative. And it was present again that morning. After several days of the cruelest temperatures, we had come to understand the Cuban heat. On that morning, it was no longer so blistering but instead, restorative, seeping into us like medicine.

"This is so nice," Casey said, admiring the small patio space. The short cement walls were painted grapefruit yellow and parrot green. The floor was stone tile. A gecko clung to a wall.

"I've named him Marcus," Graham said, emerging from his bedroom.

"Is that the same one that was on the ceiling above the bed last night?" I asked.

"Oh, yeah," he said. "We know each other well."

We took our seats at the table, and Tatiana placed small plates of fruit in front of each of us—papaya, melon, mango. She served us dark French press coffee and sweet plantains. She was barefoot and smiling.

"Ah?" she asked, hesitating through her English, her face becoming serious. "Eggs?"

"Si," I said. The boys nodded and Tatiana's smile returned.

We could hear the muted clinking of pots in the kitchen where her mother was working and a child's soft voice filling the short space between the living room and the patio. Tatiana's dark-haired daughter, maybe about five years old, sat on the floor of the narrow hallway, playing with balls on a string. Just behind her on a side table was a large framed photograph of her as an infant, dressed in white with a bow in her hair. Above it on the wall was a small wooden crucifix.

We asked for a bit more coffee.

"Best breakfast so far," I said, spreading a dab of mango preserves on a small bread roll.

The boys nodded between bites.

"Definitely best coffee," Casey said.

After a moment, Graham put down his fork. "Could you live here?" he asked.

I wasn't certain what he meant. *Could I live in this house? Could I live in Trinidad? Could I live in a place many saw as less free?* I thought maybe he was talking about the heat. *Could I live under the intense Cuban sun?*

"We've adjusted, don't you think?" I asked, knowing the answer.

"Yeah, kind of," he said. "The heat is one thing. But it's more, like, I don't know, like here, in this place, like this."

It's nearly always considered. When you visit a new place, you eventually ask yourself if it could be your home. Could you settle here? Vacation or deeper travel touring is not the best preparation for such questions. You need to inhabit a place for a time, let it soak into you, not just brush by it. A friend, who had moved a great deal for his job as a reporter, maybe every three to four years, once told me that each new place had its singular lure; it was always a mistress for a time. But then you had to go to the bank, get a haircut, do laundry, and every town he came to call home for those short stints soon felt like all the others. That seemed a dismal way to look at it. But he was probably mostly right. Still, when I visit somewhere, especially a place like Cuba—this outlawed country, alluring and mysterious—I don't think of staying. I think mostly of coming back. When I say goodbye to something—like all the houses and apartments I once lived in—I leave a piece of myself behind, something I can't have again unless I return. So, it's the returning I think about, not the staying, and what it is that I might be leaving behind.

"I think I could be here for a time, sure," I said. "The people are certainly warm."

"It is a communist country, though," Casey said, reminding us.

"The dark and menacing beast that is Communism," I said.

"We are the Federales!" Graham said, imitating the authorities we met on the beach. "May we look in your trunk?"

The boys laughed. I asked Casey to pass the coffee pot.

It was an idol question, the thought of living in Cuba, only a notion that had little real meaning. We weren't going to stay in Cuba. The boys knew that. I knew that. But it was impossible not to think about such a thing. There's this long-held belief that men are born outside their proper place. An accident of birth hurls us to our hometowns but not our homes. Instead, we travel through life, longing for a home we do not know. The streets where we grew up, the schools we attended, the travel we've embarked on are simply doors to open. It's an odd thing, but maybe the constant craving is what lunges us through our days in search of something eternal, the sojourner forever reaching for what's not there.

That afternoon we visited an open-air pottery maker's shop where the artist worked his wheel in front of photographs of Fidel Castro's long ago visit to his studio. The potter allowed Graham on the wheel for a time. "Not his first," the potter said, smiling. It wasn't. Graham had thrown bowls in high school. In Santa Clara we spent time at the Che Guevara memorial and were told to remove our hats before entering the vault where the remains of the revolutionary had been entombed. Photos of the bearded, handsome rebel lined the walls. We drove near the Bay of Pigs and saw, along the road, the simple graves of Cuban soldiers. We watched farmers drying rice on the street's hot asphalt—a common practice that drivers respected and maneuvered around—and we disputed Renaldo's claim that we were only a short distance from Havana when we were at least a three-hour drive away. There was a dinner reservation we didn't want to miss, but Renaldo appeared to be working on what we had come to call Cuban Time—an internal clock with no hands and no numbers, the principle that keeping time, some reasonable sense of schedule, was highly overrated. It was a trait we had come to understand about Renaldo and Cuba. Still, we made our dinner date, and later that night, in Old Havana, under the high colonial ceilings of the Hotel Raquel, we drank rum and smoked Montecristo cigars to commemorate the last hours in Cuba.

The next morning we had scheduled a taxi to the airport. The Plaza de San Francisco was damp from overnight showers, and the humidity was vicious. The plaza's iron chairs were wet, and the water on the seats shimmered in the hazy sun. Standing near a puddle, lapping up water, was a small dog—a street dog—one of Havana's many. We had seen the dogs each night while walking the cobblestone walkways. Dogs of similar size, weaving in and out of tourists and locals, some with ID tags the size of postcards, marked for care by an animal welfare organization. This dog, however, had no tag. It was stout, short-haired, and dirty-white. Its ears stood straight up. It looked much like the one that had befriended us earlier in the week in the plaza not far from the ancient statue of St. Francis of Assisi, the patron saint of animals. The dog had found us sitting in the plaza under steamy street lamps, and it curled up under our feet. It did not beg for food; it did not lean in, hoping to be scratched about the ear. The dog simply wanted to be near, and he stayed with us for over an hour until we left for our hotel around midnight. Maybe the morning dog was the same one from the night before. Maybe not. But it was nice to think it might have been. Like the many Cubans who had asked us about America, about baseball, reminded us of their dislike of Trump and love for Obama, and several times had implored us to stay in their country, this dog, the one that may have returned to the plaza to say goodbye, only wished to be close to something more hopeful.

As our taxi pulled away, the three of us—weary and silent—watched though the windows as Havana bumped and hustled into the day—the long lines at the bus stops, the pre-1960 American cars darting in central city traffic, a vendor selling large mangos on the corner, rainbows of laundry hanging from run-down second floor apartments, the image of Che at every turn. Everywhere that morning, like all the days before, Cubans appeared to be anticipating something, expecting some elusive change. This beautiful country—stalled in its own energy, running in place, enchanting and exasperating—was beginning to gradually stretch out from its isolation, shifting ever so slowly. It was seeking hope that something or someone would be its savior. Its people remained proud of the Cuban revolutions—the three against Spain to gain independence and the one led by Fidel Castro against a right wing, authoritarian government—and they were quick to find goodness in Guevara, the country's omnipresent spirit. But the people remained keenly aware that the hope born in these conflicts was never fully realized and because of this, Cuba is still reaching for something else, curling up under the feet of the world like the street dog, waiting to be delivered to the rest of us.

José Martí Airport was air-conditioned. Still, the thickness of the humidity clung to us, weighed us down. The terminal was busy but not crowded. The policía were present but not at every turn. The signs for the gates were in Spanish but some were also in English. A few shops sold packaged food and bottled water. Graham and I stood in a short line and checked in for our flight to Florida, just ninety miles across a thin strip of ocean. Casey's flight to Los Angeles, more than 2000 miles from Havana was scheduled for later at another terminal, so he waited for us nearby. At the currency exchange we counted our dollars and swapped the little we had left for Cuban Convertible Pesos in case we needed bottled water or to purchase some unreliable Wi-Fi time at one of the few hotspots available while waiting for our flight. And then we stood silent.

"I guess this is it," I said. I put my arms around Casey's shoulders and held tight. Graham shook his brother's hand.

It unnerved me to leave Casey alone for several hours in Havana, still having to take a cab to another terminal. I wouldn't be able to talk or text him until he reached California. Travel had been part of all of our lives, but of the three of us, Casey's travel had been the most extensive—China, Iceland, Egypt, Fiji. He had driven across America, hiking on narrow cliffs and awaking to the sunrise at the bottom of the Grand Canyon. He could more than handle a solo fifteen-minute taxi ride to Havana's terminal-3. Still, there had been that police incident near Trinidad, and although I was confident there would be no repeat of such a thing, I worried like a father.

Sun-tinged and tired, Graham turned and I walked toward our gate's security lines, rolling our carry-on bags behind us. Casey stood near the currency exchange, counting his pesos and readjusting his luggage bag. I wanted to look back to him, but I chose not to. I told myself I would see him again when he visited Chicago in a couple of months. So, instead, I walked straight ahead, letting myself relive our days as Americans in Cuba, visiting a once prohibited place. And I imagined again: Could I ever live here, as Graham had asked? I had fallen in love with this country so many years ago, and that affection had inspired longing, the melancholic desire for something unattainable and distant. There's beauty in that. So, I did not wave goodbye to Casey. I did not wave goodbye to Havana, to Cuba, to Che, to anyone or anything. There were so many reasons not to.

The Writing House

It was one day after carrying everything through the door. I sat inside my small studio—a shed in the backyard—in the quiet dusk of a Saturday among the books, photography, and art. I waited. *What happens now?* After months of filling out forms for a village permit, hauling in the shed's framework on a flatbed to the corner of our plot of property, breaking numerous jigsaw blades, nailing barn wood panels to studs, painting the ceiling, and squaring up a vinyl floor, I anticipated some magic.

I had dreamed of this day for a long time, even though at times I questioned it. *You're going to build a writer's shed? You're going to be some Henry David Thoreau wannabe?* There were those who simply smiled when I explained the not yet fully formulated plans. I'm sure some turned away to laugh. But the dream was real. And after the last of the vinyl tile was glued to the subfloor, I was proud, satisfied, and weary—a *good* weary, the kind that comes after physical accomplishment. There was soreness in my right hand from wielding a hammer—I probably was using it incorrectly—a bruise on my thumb from a misguided attempt at using a screwdriver to remove a bent finishing nail, tight back muscles from climbing up and down the ladder, and aches in my hips and thighs from squatting and stretching to meet the highest and lowest corners of the 8x10 space. There also had been outbursts, cursing miscalculated measurements. Despite the minor bang-ups and pains, there was joy. In each step of the work, I could see and feel the writer's shed—*a place of my own*—emerging. I saw myself stealing away inside in early mornings to read and write. I *was* Thoreau. I *was* Dylan Thomas in his boathouse in Wales. I *was* Henry Miller in Clichy, his artistic home. Still, looking back at this process— the planning and then building out the interior of this writer's home—I was clearly in fantasy mode. I imagined the glow of creative solace. But there I was, alone, at my desk, with evening's full darkness closing in outside, void of romance. Reality was here, and now the mysteries would begin. *Can I write here? Have I built this space only on a dream of what it might be? Have I erected my writer shed only to seduce a distorted image of artistic solitude? Have I miscalculated the value of this space, this home?*

The reality of the shed formed after meeting Leslie, falling in love, and moving to her home together after living alone in a two-flat near Chicago. After nearly two years, I asked, "Would you let me build a writer's shed?" The new home was the first place I had lived where the vision of a shed felt truly possible. Leslie gave it her blessing, even encouraged it. But then there was anxiety. It was not unlike what one experiences on the first night in a new apartment or new house. *Did I make the right move?* Your mind can't be settled. You can't sleep. You are out of place, out of sync with the dream, not to mention the apprehension of being secluded with your own thoughts. I have always considered myself someone who savored solitude, believed in its restorative power. The shed is not a cabin in the wilderness, but it is isolation nonetheless. Still, I may have underestimated what surrounded me.

I turned on the chrome lamp at my desk and looked for a book on the small shelf in the corner near the door. Gretel Ehrlich in *The Solace of Open Spaces* focuses on the American West, the vast openness she needed during a particularly tough time in her life. I love this book. I read aloud a passage I had marked with a pen long ago: "We fill up space as if it were a pie shell." I wondered if I had filled up too much. Ehrlich writes how taking away space "obstructs our ability to see what is already there." *Did I construct this writer shed on my "space" to obstruct my view? Did building it cloud my vision? Is the shed a facade for the real work of writing? Is the shed only a place to hide?*

Building a house in America is the work of ego. Make it big. Make it bold. Fill up the space with rooms, more than you need. No finished basement? That won't do. No master bath with walk-in shower? Unacceptable. What do you mean it's only a one-car garage? These perceived needs obstruct the view of a house's true and elementary purpose—to shelter and, more importantly, to nurture. The shed will shelter. There are no leaks in the roof. But I pray it will nurture, allow space for quieting the mind and soul. The shed was not built out of ego or status and certainly not simple shelter. It was built in an effort to comfort something deeper.

When first filling the space inside, I placed on my desk, a gift from Leslie—a framed watercolor of Dylan Thomas' desk in his writing shed inside the boathouse and garage along the rocks in Laugharne, Wales. Also depicted in the painting are pen and ink, journals, and scattered papers. The view is Thomas' view, out the window to the Taf Estuary and Gower Peninsula. This painting and all the photos I have seen of the poet's shed show the curtains open to the countryside, natural light pouring in. My view is north toward the wooden fence and the neighbor's back lawn. At night when the sun is long gone, I can see mostly misshapen shadows—blacks and grays.

Only a small, soft light shines from a neighbor's patio and filters through a large pine at the border of the property, reflecting off the window and into my shed. It's not enough to create a silhouette or warm the room, but it soothes nonetheless. There is no estuary or peninsula, but there is open space of a certain level, and I have given it permission to come inside.

I recently wrote a short piece about the world's most remote places. The shed and home in Laugharne were certainly not remote, not when compared to the world's most inaccessible places, or the vastness of what Ehrlich wrote about. Dylan's boathouse was walking distance from town, Brown's Hotel, and an afternoon of pints. But when inside his writing space, he was long gone. Tristan de Cunha is the most out-of-the-way inhabited archipelago in the world. It sits 1700 miles from the nearest island in South Africa. My shed is 100 feet from the back door of the house. I can see the garage from the window. But yet somehow I am distant, just on the edge of aloneness.

On the shelf to my left, I've placed a copy of Jack Kerouac's *Desolation Peak*. Big swaths of the book are taken directly from Kerouac's journal while he was a fire lookout in a cabin in the North Cascades of Washington state in the summer of 1956. For two months he was isolated on the mountain. The book is a study in seclusion, Kerouac's opportunity to be silent, to think, to write in isolation. *Desolation Peak* was his *Walden*. Just above Kerouac's book on the same shelf is Thoreau's book. A few weeks ago, I reread *Walden*, compelled to as I sawed and nailed my way through afternoons. The first time I read it, I was a high school freshman. I believe I read only parts of it. Back then I saw Thoreau's work as a nagging assignment, and the man as an old 19th century recluse who wrote silly nature stories. On my second go at it, I opened *Walden* and thumbed through. I read a passage on a dog-eared page: "I never found a companion that was so companionable as solitude." The words stung a bit. *Is my shed a place for the hermit in me? Am I only longing to be a recluse?* I leaned back in the chair and looked around. On the desk is a framed photograph of a remote boat launch in Canada. The rowboats are red and numbered. In the background are craggy mountains, fog and snow. My son, Casey took the photo. I wanted it in the shed. It speaks to the inner human need for solitude. But so many other things inside offer other things, different sides of me. On the bookshelf is a small bowl, handmade with clay and horsehair. My younger son, Graham crafted it. Tacked to the wall is a pencil drawing, flowers in a vase, the artwork of my partner's daughter, Jen. The watercolor of Thomas' shed is next to a small card with a hand-printed, two-stanza poem. "From the Sky" is the work of the poet Gary Snyder. He graciously signed it for me after I attend a reading he gave in Chicago. And there are the books scattered about—Jim Harrison and Joan Didion and Walt Whitman and Karl Ove Knausgaard. Not a lot of them, only the one's I most cherish, the ones that give me peace. I am surrounded and I am not alone, not a loner. I have created a kind of home inside these walls, a home for seclusion, yes, but also, maybe more importantly, one of shared art and love, the opposite of isolation.

Still, there are pieces missing.

I looked around again—on the desk, the shelves, in the drawer of my desk. There is nothing of my sister, nothing of my mother or father. I looked at my right hand. On the third finger I wear Dad's ring, a small diamond on onyx surrounded by gold, the ring my mother gave him when they married, the one he would never take off, that left a red indentation on his thick finger and now is making the same mark on mine. I would not have purchased such a ring for myself, but I wear it. Still, there is nothing of Dad's artwork on the shed walls, no pencil or chalk drawings. They are on the walls of the new home but not here, not in the shed, not in this place of creativity. And what about my mother? In the house, in the bottom drawer of my nightstand, is my mother's engagement ring—small diamond, platinum band, geometric metalwork. It is kept in a mustard-colored felt ring box, the box that once carried my high school graduation ring. Maybe one of my son's will use the ring for the one he loves. And under the nightstand is a hard plastic box. Inside are my sister's ashes, what's left of what has not been scattered at a football stadium and a graveyard. *Should these things be in my shed? Or am I deliberately keeping them at a distance?*

Before finding myself in the shed one evening, I read a *New York Times* article about the passing of Lou Reed. Laurie Anderson, Reed's partner in life, was donating Reed's extensive archives to the New York Public Library. She didn't want a university to have it. She thought academia would be less democratic, making it less available for those who wished to explore. Reed had left behind hundreds of recordings, notes, receipts, letters, writings, and photographs, all the things that make up an artistic life. But Anderson was saddened that despite all these meaningful remnants, the one thing that may have been most special to Reed was not there in that trove. Reed had a lifelong dedication to meditation. It weaved through his existence. It was important to him. But in all those boxes and folders, there was nothing to be found. No trace of this part of his life. What may have brought Lou Reed his most meaningful peace had vanished after his death. For Reed, meditation, it seemed, was like going home. It was where he felt the most at ease, the most real, but in the end there was no physical footprint that this cornerstone of his life ever existed.

I looked around again at all that I had brought to the shed and for what was missing. *Is this all of me? Is this it? If these things were my archives, would they say everything about me? Would it matter? Who would care?* My life will not be documented at a university or the New York Public Library, but we all want to believe that what we have done with our lives, in some way, will remain after we die. Still, so much of life, of who we really are, cannot be truly captured. It is only in our minds, stays there, and dies there. Sometimes you cannot embrace the most cherished possessions or hold on to the most important things. And maybe that's okay. There's beauty in that. It's the splendor of existence. My father and mother are gone, their true spirit gone with them. My sister—whose end came alone in a hospital emergency room bed, her body ravaged by alcohol—is a heartbreaking memory. But, so much about their lives, despite all that they meant to me, is slowly being lost in the fog of time, visible only when I'm able to fight through the haze.

I hope what happens in this shed will be captured somehow, but the truth is, much of it—like life—will be ephemeral, dissipating smoke. It is true about everything, the people we love and all the places we live, all the homes we embrace. We infinitely search for peace, for home, but the physical buildings that shelter our lives ultimately serve only as greenhouses of our being. Inside them we grow, we bloom, and soon decay and evaporate into earth and air, along with so many of those important moments—difficult and beautiful—that cannot be framed and hung on a wall, or placed on a bookshelf, or archived for all to examine. I didn't know my sister would die before I would see her one last time. I didn't know my father loved my mother so deeply until he fought so hard to live. I didn't know my mother, only in her late teens when fighting tuberculosis, was brave enough to spit at death. I didn't know my hometown was such a good place until I left it. I didn't know I would find real love again.

I stood from my desk, took a deep breath, and collected the shed's keys from the front pocket of my jeans. I turned off the lamp. I reached to close the window blind where the neighbor's light remained, but I thought again and chose to keep it open. The light was dreamlike, reassuring, like a candle or lantern showing the way. It was magical. And my shed, like all the places called home, could use a little touch of magic.

Last Home

We moved twenty bags of topsoil and a maybe as many mulch bags, rolling them to the backyard by wheelbarrow and lugging a few over my shoulder. There were bags of compost and peat moss. Gifted veteran hydrangeas had been dug out from around the perimeter of a friend's soon-to-be-renovated garage. Patriot hosta plants had been split and unearthed from an Iowa friend's garden. A rhododendron once flowering inside a decaying wooden barrel on our patio was now replanted on a mound of mulch. The purple bloom reminded me of Pennsylvania and the mountain laurel that grows in the pine forests. Much of this planting now frames the writing shed behind the house. In the front yard, we removed an overgrown Scotch pine and planted a Sargent Tina Crabapple. New pavement stones have been placed from the street to the sidewalk. And in the small garden, parallel to the house, are two new heather plants, deep crimson in color. They will melt away as the warm weather approaches. The heather struggled after the replanting, but hope remains. There's also a new tree, a dogwood, a sapling near the fence. The new earth, new plants, new trees, and new roots are like the flowers in the flowing hair of a bride. The bride is my new home, the home I have adopted, the one that will likely be my last.

There is no dread, sadness, or foreboding. It is just simply true. All the homes before—the physical ones, the metaphorical ones, or the internal homes, the ones of inner peace and certainty—have led me here, to the small, brown, brick ranch house flanked at its entrance by two towering oak trees and hugged by a sprawling magnolia in the back—the house that needed new gutters, the house that required basement work to keep the flood waters out, the house that was desperate for a new downstairs bathroom, new windows, and a freshly painted front door. Green—lime green, the green of mint, shamrocks, parakeets, the color of healing. Metaphysics says shades of lime green are the colors of renewal, the shedders of stress and worry. Colors that prove you have worked through fears and discord and now are surrounded by the energy of living, balance, and love.

"I adore your door," one neighbor told me as she walked by the home with her aging golden retriever.

"That's all Leslie," I said, taking a break from raking mulch. "Her vision, and yes, I love it, too."

In autumn sunshine, at an outside table at a winery in Virginia, over nuts and bread and olives and red wine, I offered the idea of Leslie and me moving in together. It had been only a few months since leaving Iowa, and she was just settling down in her new home after her restorative two years. I had asked her to travel with me to the town of Lovingston, Virginia where I had been asked to play a song I had written before a group of judges in a regional songwriting competition. I didn't win, and that didn't matter. The trip deepened our growing relationship, and eight months later, we parked a U-Haul truck outside my rented first floor flat near the city and loaded it up—leather chair, leather couch, a bed frame and mattress, a dresser, and books, lots of books. I had sold many things after riding a minimalism kick for a couple of years, and this made the move simple. I had also carried many possessions in my car to the house in the days before, so moving day wasn't so daunting. Still, my son and I nearly dropped a large bookcase as we maneuvered it down a set of porch stairs. With each of us holding separate ends, we started to laugh uncontrollably, re-calling another move years before when our young family had purchased a new home three blocks away from our first house. In the backyard was a twelve-foot round trampoline with a net enclosure. I dreaded the idea of disassembling dozens of parts, lugging them to the new home, and tediously putting it all back together, so I strapped skateboards to the bottom of the metal frame and rolled the trampoline down the suburban streets with the boys in it. It was a raucous ride and probably a little dangerous. That memory is what nearly caused Graham and I to lose our grips as we moved the dresser. Laughing out loud, we had to stop and regroup several times before lifting it to the truck. However, what weighed heavy that day was not what I was physically carrying, not what I was transporting in my arms.

"Are you all right?" Leslie asked.

I had stopped hauling items to the truck and had taken a seat on the front steps. In an instant, I had gone from laughing with my son to being sullen and alone.

"Damn it!" I groused. "I don't need half of this shit." The labor of packing and moving had kept me occupied and had camouflaged something else. I was leaping into a new life, and my heart had not fully caught up with my head. I wanted to move in with Leslie. I wanted to build a new life with her. I was in love and happy. But at that moment, all the moves I had ever made from home to dormitory to home to apart-ment to another home, and yet another, had begun to close in around me. Every place I had laid my head, traveled to, searched out, or embraced, surrounded me like an invading infantry. It wasn't the physical labor or too many possessions that had me brooding. That was the disguise. Instead it was the emotion of every change in my life, ones I had not fully permitted myself to acknowledge. With every home I left and every new one I entered, came a life passage; every place was like a marker on a map, and at every stop, I dragged in boxes of stuff—physical belongings, yes, but also boxes loaded with emotion. And now on this summer day with the sky threatening and the humidity building, those boxes were spilling out in front of me.

"What's going on?" Leslie asked.

"I need some time," I grumbled.

Leslie could have snapped back, told me to stop acting like a fool, told me to straighten up and refused to accept my surly attitude. She didn't deserve this. Not now. Not at this moment. It was a big day for her, too. But that is not what she did. Instead, she gave me space.

"You taking a break?" Graham asked. He had been inside the truck, adjusting the contents for more room, and had not witnessed my exchange with Leslie and the attitude swing.

"One minute," I said, turning my eyes from him. I felt tears coming, tears I didn't understand.

"Graham, let's get some of the kitchen stuff," Leslie called from the front porch.

I was alone now, a nearly full U-Haul before me, only a few more possessions left to pack, and a 13-mile drive ahead to the house where we would work for two hours—part of it in the rain—to unload a life into a house where I would empty my boxes and scatter the contents on the floor, like Halloween candy, to examine every artifact as if I were looking at them for the very first time.

Just inside the garage door of my new home, crudely stamped into the concrete floor are the imprints of a baby's bare feet—the delicate heels and the tiny toes of the right and the left. I could imagine a mother holding a child around the waist to position his little body so that his weight would allow for a careful press into damp cement. She was undoubtedly smiling, the baby laughing. Below the imprints is a name scratched with a finger or a stick into the once-wet concrete—*Billy*. And below this is a date—*8-7-45*. More than seventy years ago, a mother's small ceremony permanently observed this day, this child, and this home. I wonder now if my sons will one day think of their first home the way their parents did when all of us lived there, as a place of love and safety, as place where toes could be pressed to wet cement. It was a good house. Will they remember that? Will they think of it the same way?

The old house where I live now has good bones. It's solid and sturdy, and carries decades of lives lived with honesty. It belongs on its land. It has settled in like the old-growth trees that line the neighborhood. And until the day it is torn down to build something new and less enduring, those little toes, along with the house's bricks and concrete, and the nearly century old trees in the yard, will hold a kind of legacy. This house is supposed to be here. And I am, too. My books are on the shelves, my clothes in the closets. My prized black iron skillet is on the stove, and my omelet pan is next to her seasoned wok in one of the lower cabinets. My coffee is in the same kitchen next to her tea, and a dog rests at our feet. I am reminded of "Our House," Graham Nash's love poem to Joni Mitchell. It is a "very, very, very fine house."

I have lost my desire to search, to always be on the lookout for that special place. Whether I was aware of it or not, I have always been on the hunt for that singular spot where the heart finds its rightful cadence. My boyhood home on the street where my parents grew up, the mobile home outside Clarion State College, my first one-room apartment, my first town-home, my first four-bedroom home outside Chicago, more apartments, another townhouse, a near-city flat, and all the travel to places where I found some mystical newness—San Francisco, Navajo Nation, Paris, Cuba, even the writer's shed that now stands in the backyard have all been points on the map to this 1940s brick home in the Western Hemisphere at the latitude of 41.799, the longitude of -87.969, 22.6 miles from Chicago's Loop, 1329 miles from Havana, 1481 miles from Window Rock, Arizona, the capitol city of the Navajo Nation, and some 4143 miles from Ernest Hemingway's first apartment in France at 113 Rue Notre-Dame-des-Champs.

The last home has echoes of the first. The architecture is different—from a Cape Cod to a ranch, one on a hill and the other on the flattest of land—but they are similar in size, both about 1200 square feet in all. Both have been cared for and lived in with attention and comfort. Christmases have been celebrated, birthdays recognized, toasts have been made. Laughter has resounded inside their walls. Tears have seeped into plaster. Arguments have erupted in their rooms, but forgiveness has overcome. There has been sickness and healing. Quiet meditation has complemented a party's roar. Tea has been brewed, coffee pressed, pancake breakfasts served for six, for eight, for ten. Expensive cabernet has filled delicate stemware, and everyday reds have been poured in juice glasses. Beer from bottles and the smoke of cigars have mixed with smoldering patio fires. Pies have been made. Roasts roasted. Salmon has been charred in black pans. Thai stir-fry has simmered in a wok. Dogs have lost their battles with age in the basement of the Cape and on the kitchen floor of the ranch—good dogs, dogs born to family. Hearts have been stolen, broken, and restored. Colors of paint have splashed the walls. Furniture rearranged. Photographs have been taken, framed, and hung on walls. Closets cleaned. Leaks repaired. Children have learned to walk and eventually run to what they could call their own. Music has filled the spaces—rock and jazz and folk and opera. The live notes of guitars and piano, the thump and rattle of drums and tambourine have accompanied the gentle and the sneering, singing voices of the young and the old. And in the deep hours, solace has embraced both homes even when the occupants were not so certain what they wanted today would be there tomorrow. And in the front yard of the old, there was my mother's favorite lilac bush, the clematis that clung to the fence, the Japanese maple that blossomed near the driveway. In the backyard were the apple tree, the cherry tree that offered the kind of fruit birds feasted on, and the thick goldenrod that lined the south end of the lot line. And in the middle of the garden, near the porch, was my mother's favorite, a red rose bush that she pruned and watered religiously. It was easy to envision my boyhood home after watering the newest home's freshest plantings, after putting away shovels and rakes, after the heat of the midday sun gave way to evening coolness, after growing weary from the toils in the dirt. From the past to the present, from one garden to another, roots have begotten roots and old earth—made rich by the decaying of what could not remain—has nurtured something new. That evening's blue and distant horizon reminded me that there is something always far away, out of reach, and that longing is a lifetime. But no matter, the stars in the sky remain essentially unchanged, and heaven—twisted only by the seasons—hangs above the new home and the old as it always has and always will.

Acknowledgements

Thank you, Leslie O'Hare. Thank you, Casey and Graham.

I am also grateful to Columbia College Chicago for allowing me to take time away to write, redraft, and write again this book, the Chicago Writers Association for their continued support, the Ernest Hemingway Foundation of Oak Park, and the Jack Kerouac Project of Orlando, Florida.

About the Author

David W. Berner is a memoirist whose personal stories tell all of our stories. His memoirs reflect on our collective relationships and how those experiences link us to the world we share. From stories of fathers and sons, to road trips, travel memoir, pets, and music, David's books are mirrors of our common human experience.

Storytelling has been a part of David's life since his days as a young boy, delivering The Pittsburgh Press newspaper. He began telling his own stories and the stories of others as a reporter for numerous radio stations, including freelance work at National Public Radio and more recently for CBS in Chicago.

David's reporting background has given birth to award-winning memoirs and novels based on his own experiences.

He has been the Writer-in-Residence for the Jack Kerouac Project in Orlando, where he was privileged to live and work at the Kerouac House in Orlando for two-and-a-half months. He later was honored with the Writer-in-Residence position at the Ernest Hemingway Birthplace Home in Oak Park, Illinois.

"To all the readers who have found my work relevant to their lives, I am forever grateful."

David W. Berner is the author of four previous memoirs: *Accidental Lessons*, which won the 2011 Royal Dragonfly Grand Prize for Literature; *Any Road Will Take You There*, which won the 2013 Chicago Writers Association Book of the Year Award for Indie Nonfiction; *There's a Hamster in the Dashboard: A Life in Pets*, which was honored as a 2015 Book of the Year by *Chicago Book Review; and October Song,* which won the 2017 Golden Dragonfly Grand Prize for Literature. He is also the author of two novels: *Night Radio*, and *A Well-Respected Man.* David has been the Writer-in-Residence at the Jack Kerouac Project in Orlando, Florida, and at the Ernest Hemingway Birthplace in Oak Park, Illinois. He lives outside Chicago.

Made in the USA
Columbia, SC
07 April 2019